Joseph J. Spae, c.i.c.m.

CHURCH AND CHINA: TOWARDS RECONCILIATION?

Chicago 1980 Leuven

THE CHICAGO INSTITUTE OF THEOLOGY AND CULTURE

Copyright: The Chicago Institute of Theology and Culture

ISBN: 0-936078-01-4

All orders must be prepaid.

For additional copies please send check for
US $10.00 or Belgian Francs 300, or the
equivalent in your currency

to

Joseph J. Spae, cicm,
Dennenlaan 8,
B-3031 OUD-HEVERLEE
Belgium   Tel.:(016) 22 93 16

Allow up to one month or more for postal delivery. Overseas
copies will be sent by surface mail unless airmail is request

This is the first European edition.

Translations are in preparation.

TABLE OF CONTENTS

+ + +

THIS BOOK IS DEDICATED

to

ALL CHINESE CHRISTIANS

"THAT THEY MAY BE ONE"

+ + +

PREFACE

Much has happened since the death of Mao, and much has been written the last twelve months about "normalization" of China's relations withe the western world, and with the Church. For sheer theological reasons, China remains Christianity's monumental challenge of the century. One billion Chinese face one billion Christians. Together Christians and Chinese make up half of all the men and women for who, the Lord Jesus shed his blood. Both groups need one another; both are jointly committed to partnership for human happiness. Yet they have stood tragically divided during the last thirty years. The quantity and quality of all involved underscores the tragedy of this division. It also indicates the magnitude of the task ahead.

In the pages which follow, I intend to inventory some efforts on either side, the Christian and the Chinese, to come to grips with this challenge. In doing so I shall impose upon myself a fivefold limitation: 1. I write from a theological perspective, by which I mean that a Christian concern and reflection underlie my approach; 2. I write from a Roman Catholic point of view, which means that, while remaining fully cognizant of our ecumenical task, I strongly believe in the mission and the service of Catholicism to the Chinese people; 3. I almost esclusively draw on sources, printed and oral, which bdcame available during 1979, and I shall only guard their confidentiality when required; 4. In the use of these sources, I shall give priority to official and semi-official publications, such as the People's Daily and the Beijing Review; 5. I freely admit the abysmal ignorance under which even so-called China experts labor, according to John K. Fairbank's well-known dictum: "A China expert who does not feel ignorant is a fool." Hence I welcome fraternal corrections, and, in preparation for a sequel to this book, further pertinent information.

I want to thank my friend and colleague Robert Schreiter for his contribution to this volume. My sincere thanks also go to people around the world who helped me write this book but prefer to remain anonymous.

January 6, 1980
Feast of the Wise Men from the East   J.S.

-- All dates are 1979 unless otherwise noted --

PRAYER FOR CHINA AND FOR THE CHURCH

Lord our God, Father of all people, we think with great
interest and understanding of the 1000-million Chinese
throughout the world. For them, as for all of us, You are
the truth, the way, and the life. It is You whom unawares
they seek. It is You whom they miss when their efforts
for justice, equality and peace are defeated.

We pray for all men and women, young and old, who suffer
under the scourges of earthquakes, social dislocation and
hidden grief. We pray especially for all those who are
despised for the sake of your Son's name.

Give us, dear Father, to recognize the good wherever
people are good. Forgive us and our Church for our lack
of understanding, love and respect, toward the Chinese people.

Give your Church that unity and that charity without
which the Chinese people could not recognize us as your
children, and as the disciples of your Son.

Give that, if it is your will, even in our day, we may
build together with the people of China a new world and a
new earth, the sign and the reality of that blessedness to
which You have called us all. Through Christ, your Son and
our Lord, who gave His life that we might live.   J. S.

The author wrote this prayer when the Tangshan
earthquake was announced. The earthquake occur-
ed on July 28, 1976. It had a magnitude of 7.8
on the Richter scale. According to BR, 12/28,
242,000 people were killed and 164,000 seriously injured.

INTRODUCTION

THE CHINESE PAST AS FUTURE: A NEW INVENTORY

At the pace Church-and-China news hit the religious headlines during 1979, this inventory will be fairly outdated by the time the printer's ink is dry. This is all to the good because immobilism in China-Church relations can only prolong an unbearable situation.

We know that, for Mao and his followers, it is the capitalist world that constitutes a world of darkness. Communists claim that they will overturn that world and transform it "into a world of light such as previously never existed." (Mao Zedong, "On Practice," 1937) The People's Republic of China (PRC) set out valiantly to realize that dream, though with what measure of lasting success remains to be seen. Rarely, if ever, has such an ambitious attempt been made to quickly change the living patterns of one of the greatest nations on earth. While it is true that the men who played the largest role in shaping the Chinese Communist Party were outspokenly hostile toward the Chinese "feudal tradition," it is equally true that they were willing to accept some elements, as Mao put it, "even from the culture that existed in capitalist countries during the period of Enlightenment." Recent events seem to prove that the Chinese leadership is far too intelligent to abandon China's cultural tradition. The anti-Confucius campaign is already muted, and since 1977 the Master's birthday has been celebrated with popular fairs. Kuo Moruo, the archaeologist who later became a vice-premier, has honored him "as the champion of the rights of the people and a fomenter of armed rebellion."

Nevertheless, the more than a quarter-century shock treatment administered to the Chinese people and their traditional institutions makes it virtually impossible to return to the pre-1949 type of society. To many, even the changes since 1976 seem irreversible, a fact, many hope, that could turn to the advantage of an acceptable contact in the early eighties between China and the Church.

The transcendental aspect has been an outstanding feature of Chinese religious life. This implies a community effort to guide people toward their temporal happiness. Traditionally, the best of Chinese religiosity is built upon a belief in gods and spirits, and on the sacredness of a world order which calls for rituals related to the beyond. The commun-

ist attack on religion is precisely an attack on the beyond-
ness of religion. This is the aspect which PRC officials
call "superstition."

In China, religion has always been more diffused than organized or functional. In many ways China's Three Religions,
Confucianism, Buddhism and Taoism, are non-theistic, non-ex-
clusive ways of life. An integration of many past religious
strains, to which Christianity and Maoism must now be added,
is already for the Chinese masses an accomplished fact, un-
related, and even inimical to any religious belonging. The
holistic structure of today's Chinese society performs, often
adequately, many basic psychological functions which traditionally were reserved for theistic religions, such as Islam
and Christianity. Small wonder then that recent theological
research indicates that Maoism is a sociopolitical doctrine
which advocates a style of life with unmistakable religious
overtones. It has become far from easy to distinguish between
what is "Chinese" and what is "Maoist" (or, for that matter,
"Marxist" or Christian) in Chinese life.

Many observers claim that, at present, the traditional aspects of Chinese religiosity reappear, although subconscious-
ly and in a changing social setting. Instead of the age-old
cohesion of the family, particularly kept alive through an-
cestor worship, Maoism stresses "the unity of the masses,"
and "the integration of the local community." Both these
principles serve as a new type of extensive kinship. In part,
biological relatedness is being replaced by ideological af-
finity. There is not as much novelty in this recent trend as
meets the eye. China has always had a profusion of pseudo-
kinship groups, some of them secret, others more directly
inspired by religious beliefs, but all of them stressing the
sacred duty to render mutual assistance within the group.

It would be entirely in keeping with the traditional tone
of Chinese religiosity if a psychologically accepted paral-
lelism were struck between the cultic role of the Emperor
and that of Mao's successors; between the Mandate of Heaven,
exalted by Confucianism, and the rulings which come down
from the Communist Party. Hence one can view Maoism as a
quasi-religion, or as an ethico-political system which is
supportive of an all-embracing statecraft, or again, as an
ideology which calls for the submission of all religious
yearnings to its dictatorial goals. Thereby the Chinese traditional control of religion is continued -- one might think
here of the Board of Rites, the Li-pu of the Qing dynasty --
only more brutally, because now enforced by a modern government which arrogates to itself the interpretative monopoly
of what religion should do.

While there is little room in the PRC for private religious

choice, Chinese history proves that oppressive measures against religion were relatively ineffective. One feels that this phenomenon may repeat itself, also today and also in the case of Christianity. Zhou Enlai had a point when he said, in an interview with Rajah B. Manikam, bishop of the Tamil Evangelical Lutheran Church in South India: "We have no scientific basis to predict the future of religion. Religion may continue for all time or it may simply disappear. Only the future can tell." Hence the longterm outcome of Communist dominance over religion is far from certain. This fact should bring a ray of hope, not only to Christians, but to the majority of the Chinese people as well.

I intend to approach the subject of Church-and-China relations with all the realism at my command. But this realism is salted with Christian hope. I watch China events with love for the Chinese people, and with empathy for those who rule their nation. I find no room for facile comparisons between what enthusiastic visitors have called "fervor in the service of the people" over against "a lack of social-mindedness" which some associate with the Christian rank and file. Mao's "to serve the people" certainly has religious overtones, but only God probes the inner devotion of the heart. What with the scarcity of controllable information, one should   know more about the permissible degree of personal and corporate freedom before sitting in judgment on the quality of spiritual life in the PRC. I hesitate therefore to endorse Solzhenitsyn's guess that China is one huge Gulag Archipelago. But I equally demur when Joseph Needham calls the PRC "the only true Christian country in the world." No doubt, befitting the Middle Kingdom, truth lies somewhere between these two extremes. And that truth shall make us free of prejudice.

Recent sociological research on Church growth tends to show that religious behavior is often most intense among the working-class. This parameter is re-inforced by the fact that the attraction of an ultimate meaning system is not due as much to its ideological content as to its overall inner appeal. Such an appeal betrays many characteristics of true religious experience because it has a seriousness, a costliness, and a strictness of its own. Many feel that there is such an appeal in Chinese society today. And they connect it with the recovery of human dignity. If this be so, one may approvingly conclude that the Chinese people is being led to new forms of dedication based on communal consent rather than on individual choice. But, again, one wishes to know more about the facts. To repeat our question: What is the degree of freedom in Chinese society which assures the humaneness of their style of life? Or, in other words, what price national dignity?

China's past and the irreversible nature of her present evolution are the twin pillars of her epochmaking challenge to the Church. "Challenge," in Chinese means both danger and opportunity. When seriously challenged, the Chinese say: "Push forward in the face of a hundred difficulties!" 百折不挠. This advice aptly applies to all efforts at reconciliation between China and the Church worthy of theology.

CHRISTIAN MISSION AMONG THE CHINESE PEOPLE: WHERE DO WE GO FROM HERE?

The first issue that will have to be faced by American Christians is an open and sympathetic appraisal of the achievements that chracterize the People's Republic of China. The Chinese government has restored to the people their pride, dignity, and self-confidence. After one hundred years of humiliation this is in itself a remarkable achievement.

A second area that I believe deserves careful attention when Christians meet is the price that has been paid for these achievements. I am sure there will be no way for such a dialogue to get under way unless American Christians are prepared to consider with Chinese Christians the price that is required by their own, that is, American, prosperity and affluence. I think Chinese Christians will want to talk about this. This includes the unemployment, the high inflation, the exploitation of foreign markets, the labor cost in production of American goods in other parts of the world, and how that undergirds United States prosperity.

Anyone who has followed the developments within the PRC these last thirty years, and has had the privilege of being there, cannot escape the authoritarian characteristics of their national life. The pressures for conformity are overwhelming. Primarily they come from peer pressure. However, when peer pressure does not work, there are the farms and indoctrination centers. Where that does not work, there is prison and even execution. This is part of the record that has to be examined. If a fair appraisal is to be made of the achievements of these past thirty years, the issues of human rights and religious freedom cannot be put aside.

Tracey K. Jones, Jr., General Secretary of the United Methodist Board of Global Ministries, New York, in Occasional Bulletin, July 1979.

PART ONE:

THE CHINA THAT CONFRONTS THE CHURCH IN 1980

―――――――――――――――――――――――――――
―――――――――――――――――――――――――――

   At the beginning of 1979 I spent three exciting weeks in
Hong Kong and Taiwan on a fact-finding mission related to
the new-new China. At that time the local papers crowded
their pages with China reports and editorially complained
that they could hardly keep up with the news, let alone
explain what all this meant. Three words expressed the
prevailing mood: change, normalization, and hope. Let me
try to plumb the implications of these words at the hand
of a variety of little facts which were busily making big
history.

   Less than thirty months after Mao's death on September
9, 1976, China has changed in a fundamental and irreversible
way. From the left course of the Cultural Revolution
(1966-76), the new leaders have made an unexpected U-turn
to the right. On October 6, 1976, Hua Guofeng arrested the
Gang of Four. He brought back to office leaders who had
been sacked and humiliated. The most important among them
was Deng Xiaoping who became Vice-premier. Hua also convened
the Fifth National People's Congress, February 26-March 5,
1978. This Congress approved a revised and liberalized
Constitution which aims at promoting "the four modernizations."

Chapter 1:

"A long journey begins with a few careful steps."

THROUGHOUT 1979 economic change dominates the national scene. Maoist humdrum managers are replaced by better-trained technicians. Work rules provide bonuses as incitement to greater output. Salaries are raised by as much as 40% for the first time in fifteen years. All these innovations were former heresies. The creed of self-reliance is abandoned in favor of soliciting US$600-billion in long-term investments in factories, training centers, hotels, arms and... Coca-cola. China will pay her huge debt to the outside world by goods produced in 51/49% jointly owned and operated production ventures. The 500.000 visitors of 1978 are followed by 4-million others in 1979. As Deng told the Americans: "All are invited to come, see and compare!"

On January 1, the word normalization is launched into political and religious orbit. It is quickly spreading to all sectors of public life. Mao's dictum about "intellectual young people must be educated by farmers" turns out to be a cruel ruse invented by the Gang of Four. Many intellectuals and artists are taken off the list of "nine stinkers" to which they had been relegated together with landlords, rich farmers, anti-revolutionists, criminals, rightists, rebels, spies and capitalist roaders. From 1966 to 1977, no students were admitted to higher institutions. As Deng said correctly: "We lost a generation of scientists." In 1978, 8000 students were admitted to the universities. In 1979, out of 4.6-million applicants 270.000 were enrolled. Examinations regain respectability. The official view set forth by Premier Hua in a TV-interview with Felix Greene, September 11, sounds as follows:

Some people had the misunderstanding that an important element of the revolution in education was opposition to examinations. Examinations are an acceptable means to help students and stimulate them in their studies. Comrade Mao Zedong was never against examinations as such. He was only against such uncalled-for methods

of examination as deliberately trying to baffle students
or take them by surprise. The Gang of Four considered
it a "heroic act" to turn in a blank paper at examinations
and made much publicity about it. (BR, 10/19:11; 10/12:6)

Premier Hua admits in the same interview that "our relatively undeveloped economy does not, as yet, allow us to build
institutions of higher learning in sufficient numbers so as
to permit all our young people to receive a higher education."
On the number of Chinese students now studying abroad we have
this authoritative information:

China has sent 2,230 scholars and students to 33 countries
during the last 22 months... Among those who have gone
abroad, 180 are postgraduates and 420 are undergraduates.
About 1,800 major in natural science and 400 in social
science and languages... There are at present Chinese
students all over the world: 500 in the United States,
300 in Britain, 200 each in France and the Federal Republic of Germany, and 100 in Japan. There are also Chinese
students and scholars in Algeria, Australia, Belgium,
Canada, Denmark, Italy, the Democratic People's Republic
of Korea, Kuwait, Mexico, the Netherlands, New Zealand,
Norway, Romania, Sweden, Switzerland and Yugoslavia...
Some governments and organizations have granted scholarships to hundreds of Chinese students. (BR, 11/23:7)

In fact, the Katholieke Universiteit van Leuven has offered
twenty scholarships, soon to be raised to eighty, an offer
which was enthusiastically accepted by Bejing. A KUL team
under Vice-Rector Herman Servotte visited there in September
and was told: "It's cheaper to educate our students in Belgium than in China."

Normalization in various degree also extends to the religious field, as I shall show below. There are reports about
churches being opened and restored in the major cities where
foreign consulates will be established in 1980.

The standard visitor to China is shown the standard places.
An average visit covers five major cities and a few communes,
of which there are 50,000. Opportunities for free conversation with the people are rare at best; sometimes they are
publicly discouraged. But in these and many other things it
is impossible to generalize. Most visitors, and particularly
those who have known pre-Mao China, come back impressed.
They tell of a China which, in Deng's words, is still "a
poor and backward country," but which, at the same time, is
very proud of its achievements.

This pride is understandable. When I went to China in 1937,
I saw hundreds of beggars in the streets of Beijing. In

Tianjin I saw hundreds of women and children for sale, driven away from the land by famine. In the PRC of today visitors observe no extremes of poverty and wealth. People look happy; they are reasonably well housed, dressed and fed. This is a remarkable achievement which does great credit to the country. Certainly, peasant life remains hard. There still are hundreds of communes without electricity or mechanization. But plans to remedy this situation exist, and there is progress everywhere.

The Chinese people display a strong collective spirit which is the envy of the West. They are justifiedly proud of their commitment to community achievements reached at a leisurely pace and free of the frenetic competitiveness which is endemic in our consumerist societies. There are no advertisements, at least until quite recently. Work is allocated according to national needs but without much freedom of personal choice There are few private cars. There are millions of bicycles.

There are recent, semi-official, reports on an upsurge of crime in the major cities: "Recently, social order in some cities has been unsatisfactory and there has been an increase of criminal offenses. This must be curbed."(B.R., 12/7:3)

> The causes of criminal activities are many, the chief being the pernicious influence of the ultra-Left line which was rife for many years in the past and which has not yet been completely eliminated. Some of the criminals were so-called "rebels against capitalist-roaders." They were in the habit of "beating, smashing and looting. Now they are creating disturbances under the signboard of "democracy and freedom" in a vain attempt to seize political power in chaos. (BR, 12/21:6)

The same source (11/2:18-24) published a long feature article on teenage delinquents. We learn that there are ten reformatories in Beijing, housing 1,423 juvenile delinquents. For all that, visitors report that in China theft is rare and that belongings can be left safely in hotels.

People are friendly and courteous, and quite willing to talk through interpreters. There is general concern for the welfare of all and for the world at large. We can all learn from the Chinese experience in health, education and child care. This favorable situation offsets the pressure to conform, the strictures on individual freedom, the din of propaganda, and the uncertainty of the future. Christian observers point out that, in China, many Gospel values are taught and practised, such as helping others, unselfish sharing, detachment from wealth and comfort, and a willingness to make serious sacrifices for the common good.

Yet, in the same breath, the official press also reports signs of increasing unrest and protest. There is (or rather, there was) Beijing's 150-meter long Democracy Wall and its notorious posters. In fact, the constitutional freedom to post dazibao, once encouraged by Mao himself, remained only effective from November 1978 until March 1979. Since then many posters lacked spontaneity. They either advertised the Party line or hinted at rifts within the Party. Thus we have recently seen some posters which supported Deng Xiaoping -- who christened the wall at Xidan "Democracy Wall" in an interview with American columnist Robert Novak last year -- while thereby obliquely denouncing Premier Hua. One poster cited the example of Watergate and suggested that even "big shots" could be dethroned. A man who attempted to defend Chairman Mao against low ratings on a poster was roundly beaten up. Police did nothing to save him from the anger of the crowd.

There is much talk in the posters about human rights. Beijing papers, on February 5, mentioned that groups of peasants protested, in front of Hua's residence, against "the evil of communes which keep us starved and deny our rights." A sad comment on the event: these peasants were left to die in the bitter winter night.

Then too, there is the rising and ebbing tide of "freedom swimmers." Asiaweek, 11/16, reports:

> A quarter-million refugees have fled from China into Hong Kong during the past eighteen months. In October alone 12,000 illegal immigrants from China were caught. Upwards of 1,000 were seized in one 24-hour period... The story is more astonishing for its apparent impact on governments and good samaritans across the world who are agitated over the refugees exodus from Vietnam. No one is asking why masses of people in China are so desperate to flee their country.

Obviously the tap of refugees can be turned on and off at will. After Margaret Thatcher protested to visiting Chairman Hua, the traffic suddenly stopped and the Hong Kong government duly reported "no arrests for two consecutive days." The Chinese government seems to encourage the departure of some types of undesirable citizens. At the same time punishments for abetting emigration have become extremely harsh. A Canton court condemned the master of a fishing boat to 30 years in prison, while the new Penal Code provides only one year jail sentences for organizing illegal emigration. At present "criminals who sneak across the border to foreign countries," as they are called in recent instructions of the Canton authorities, are often packed off to remote provinces and never heard of again.

I have mentioned the new Penal Code and the matter of
human rights. As the concept and the administration of law
is vital to future Church-and-China relations something
more must be said about it.

The Second Session of the Fifth National People's Congress
(NPC) met in Beijing from June 18 to July 3, concurrently
with the Second Session of the Chinese People's Political
Consultative Conference. The NPC meeting was attended by
3,279 members out of a total of 3,497 deputies drawn from
all walks of life and representing all 55 national minorities as well as overseas Chinese and compatriots from Hong
Kong, Macao and Taiwan. The event hopefully marked two
steps forward for the protection of human rights, a fact
which was proudly mentioned by Premier Hua and by Ye Jianying, Chairman of the NPC Standing Committee, who at 86 is
one of the most powerful men in China.

Hua candidly admitted past failures of leadership. In his
words: "We are working steadily to institutionalize our
democracy and perfect our legal system. But we want our
friends to know that we oppose anarchism and the use of
democracy for the purposes of infringing upon the rights of
others." Hua then called for the "three don'ts": 1. Don't
pick on people for their faults; 2. Don't put labels on
people; and 3. Don't use a big stick (repression and persecution) against people who have differing opinions.

Ye's 2-hour speech has been interpreted in the foreign
press as the most outspoken criticism from the Party top
of the Party bureaucracy, the failings of the economy, and
the shortcomings of Chairman Mao. There were remarkable
highlights in his speech, such as this:

> In education in the ideological line we must get down
> to realities and not conduct it in a formalistic way.
> We must proceed from the objective state of affairs and
> tackle actual problems which remain unsolved owing to
> failure of emancipating the mind ... Emancipating the
> mind means studying and respecting objective laws and
> acting in accordance with these laws.

Here precisely is the rub. The NPC proposed and accepted
the implementation of seven new laws. The new Code of Criminal Procedure is a revision of drafts worked out before
the Cultural Revolution. It puts emphasis on the right of
persons to have legal counsel; it stresses evidence of guilt
versus confession as a means of reaching a verdict. One
problem recognized by the Chinese leadership is the fact
that China has few trained lawyers, perhaps not more than
three to four hundred. Another problem is the possibility
that the new legal changes, if they are to go beyond words,

may give rise to conflicts of interest between the Party
and the people. It must be remembered that, officially,
the people have sofar been the only source of law. It remains therefore to be seen how the new Code will reflect
upon the work of the People's Courts. According to the new
Minister of Justice, Wei Wenbo, 74, "The task of these
courts is part of the administrative work of the state and
should therefore come under the unified management of judicial administrative organs." (BR, 1/12; 10/5:7-31; 10/12:9)
Obviously, the allocation of judicial powers between Party
and people might become a knife cutting both ways in matters
of human rights and local autonomy.

One of the difficulties we face in the interpretation of
all news from China is the apparent discrepancy between
words and facts. In such a vast country no uniformity need
be found. Rather some confusion due to the variety of time
and place must be sympathetically accepted. The Chinese
people themselves fully share our foreign perplexity. This
explains their reticence when questioned, and their often
fatalistic outlook upon an uncertain future.

Sporadically the curtain of silence is pierced by the
voice of dissidents. Everybody, in China and abroad, has
heard of Wei Jingsheng, 29, the zoo electrician whose sole
crime seems to have been that he wanted to engage the Party
in debate over a fifth modernization, that of democracy.
On March 29, Wei was arrested. He was found guilty on October 16 of "counterrevolutionary agitation and supplying a
foreigner with military intelligence." He was sentenced to
15 years in prison. On November 6, the Beijing High Court
ratified this verdict, against which there is no appeal.

A taped transcript of Wei's trial shows that he went down
in a noble burst of rhetoric: "Those who won't allow criticism of Marxism are not Marxists. Everybody has the right
to follow what he thinks are correct thoughts. One cannot
use the law to impose one's beliefs on others." Wei scoffed
at the charge of being called a counterrevolutionary by
those "who feel that to follow whatever the current leader
says, is revolutionary." He chided the persecution: "During
the rule of the Gang of Four everything was considered
secret. Does the prosecution still want people to follow
this tradition?" (BR,10/26:6; 11/16:15-6; CSM,10/23; SFC,
10/2; IHT, 11/14)

According to eyewitnesses arrests at Democracy Wall were
performed "at the whim of the police." This is unlikely. On
November 3, when Wei's friend Liu Qing, an editor of the
April Fifth Forum (thus named after the 1976 demonstrations
in Tienanmen Square in honor of the late Premier Zhou Enlai)

was selling copies of the unofficial transcript of the trial, 50 policemen swooped down and arrested four persons. Mr Liu fled in the confusion but later gave himself up to the police feeling responsible for the detention of others. The police told him they had acted on orders and did not have to explain.

I would want to be the last one to exaggerate the importance of Democracy Wall or the influence of dissidents of any hue in China. Yet the government's violent reaction to a few hundred protesters betrays its fear that their views might be shared by millions of disgruntled youths who have dared dream of a freedom different from the one they now enjoy. That freedom, symbolized by Democracy Wall, was always in jeopardy. Access to the Xidan Wall is now forbidden. Another site, the only one in the capital, was opened in Yuetan or Moon Altar Park. On December 6, the Beijing Municipal Revolutionary Committee issued provisional instructions on putting up big-character posters in the city:

1. All big- or small-character posters are to be put up at a site in Moon Altar Park. Posting them at Xidan Wall or any other public place is prohibited.

2. A registration center is to be set up near the site for those who wish to put up posters to register their names, pseudonyms, addresses and units to which they belong. The contents of the posters will not be examined.

3. Writers of big-character posters will be held responsible for the political and legal implications of the contents. It is forbidden to disclose state secrets, fabricate information, make false charges, libel others and conduct other activities that violate the law.

4. Those who create disturbances or riots at the site will be duly punished according to law. (BR,12/7&14)

Certainly, this does not mean the end of freedom of expression for the Chinese people. At the Fourth National Congress of Chinese Writers and Artists in Beijing, October 30-November 16, Vice-premier Deng invited his audience of 3,200 "to let a hundred flowers bloom and a hundred schools contend." (BR,11/9:3-4) This, of course, is Mao's famous phrase which is also found on an 8-fen commemorative stamp issued at that occasion. Deng, it would seem, used Mao's words in memory of those who took them seriously only to lose life and limb under the Gang of Four.

Wei and many other dissidents deified Mao only a few years ago. Now they feel betrayed by him and his successors. Shipped to the countryside they had worked hard, in the Chairman's words, "for the good of the people." What they found there sometimes was ineptitude and corruption. Such was the young man who told a <u>CSM</u> correspondent:

> We are the victims of the Cultural Revolution. How do I know that my ideas are right, unless I have a chance to pit them against others, unless I can read freely, listen freely, discuss freely? All I know at this point is how little I know. We young people hunger for knowledge. We thirst for beauty. (12/17)

This young man and millions of Chinese youths do not reject Mao Thought, or communism. But they belong to the lost generation that was seared by the Cultural Revolution. And they are no longer inclined to accept any doctrine because of some pronouncement from Beijing officials who, they feel, are out of touch with the harsh reality of their lives.

VICE-PREMIER DENG ON LITERATURE AND ART

It is imperative to continue to adhere to the orientation set forth by Comrade Mao Zedong that art and literature should serve the masses, particularly the workers, peasants and soldiers, and uphold the principles of "letting a hundred flowers blossom and a hundred schools of thought contend," or "making the past serve the present and foreign things serve China," or also "weeding through the old to bring forth the new." The umhampered development of different forms and styles in creative work and free discussion of different viewpoints and schools of thought in literary and art theories should be encouraged.

The people should judge for themselves whether the ideological content and artistic expression of a literary and art work should not be realized by issuing administrative orders; deviations in this respect should be eliminated. The question of what to write and how to write can only be solved gradually by the artists themselves through practice.

> Deng Xiaoping in a speech at the opening ceremony of the Fourth National Congress of Writers and Artists, Beijing, October 30, 1979. (<u>BR</u>,11/9)

Chapter 2:

The demythologization of Mao

On October 1, the Chinese people celebrated the 30th anniversary of the PRC. The joy and glamor of the occasion are summed up in this paragraph:

> Well-stocked stores with a rich variety of goods, blooming flowers in the parks and big red lanterns hanging over the gates of many buildings added to the joyous atmosphere as the capital's 8-million people celebrated their National Day. (BR,10/5)

Many readers of the PRC's best-known English periodical were struck by the fact that this semi-official account of the solemnities did not mention the name of Chairman Mao. The Museum of the Chinese Revolution, the BR tells us, hosted an exhibition on the history of the Democratic Revolution, 1921-49. At the opening of this exhibition (a matter not mentioned by the BR) Liu Shaoqi, one of Mao's most vigorous and long-accursed opponents, was quietly rehabilitated. On a huge banner he could be seen in the company of Zhou Enlai, the beloved Premier, and of Marshal Zhu De, Mao's longtime companion in arms.

Whatever happened to Mao? He is still in his crystal tomb, enbalmed in the rectangular mausoleum on Tienanmen. The mausoleum was closed to the public from January to May "for repairs," althoughthere was hardly any sight of them. It has now reopened on certain days of the week. In hushed silence and in reverence, thousands of people come to view the Great Helmsman. Do they still carry him in their hearts? I think they do.

Yet, there is no doubt about this fact: during recent months, although Mao Thought is still mentioned, it is no longer a fabao 法寶, "a magic weapon," which was the code word used during the Cultural Revolution. Fact is, during 1979 Mao was officially reduced to mortal size. When I was in Hong Kong in 1978, some bookshops were fairly paved with the Little Red Book, so-called because of its red

plastic cover. Its real title is <u>Quotations from Mao Zedong</u>.
The little book exists in 36 languages and nearly one-billion
copies were printed since the first edition came out during
the Cultural Revolution. When I returned to Hong Kong in
June, I had to look almost under the counter to find a copy.
And for good reason. We now know that the Little Red Book,
once considered "a model book in which every sentence is
truth," was in fact an ignoble ruse of Lin Biao to ridicule
the Chairman:

> Besides absolutizing and canonizing Mao Zedong Thought,
> besides referring to it as the product of the brain of
> a genius and disclaiming that it too must be subjected
> to test in practice, for many years Lin Biao and the
> Gang of Four did their utmost to create an air of mys-
> tery about the leader and incited a kind of religious
> fanaticism, so much so that they were simply trying to
> bring people back to the age of ignorance. Where can
> we find an iota of Marxism in this! (<u>BR</u>,11/23)

The standard quotation to prove this point is taken from
a 1949 address of Zhou Enlai to a Youth League congress:
"Mao was the most eminent of the leaders of the Chinese revolution, but he was only one among many. He was a man and
not a god."

Marshal Ye, in the 30th Anniversary speech to which I
have already referred, puts the same matter in an even more
definitive key. Be it remarked that this speech, according to an official Communique of the Fourth Plenary Session
of the 11th Central Committee of the Communist Party, dated
September 28, "was submitted for discussion to the Plenary
Session... and is a historic document of great importance,
one to guide the work of the whole Party, the whole army and
the whole country for a long period." From this memorable
speech I lift the words which follow:

> Comrade Mao criticized himself in his speech at the
> Central Work Conference in 1962 attended by 7,000
> people... We had to pay a bitter price for our mis-
> takes committed during the first 17 years after the
> founding of the People's Republic. Instead of avoiding
> errors which could have been avoided, we committed
> even more serious ones... Lin Biao and the Gang of Four
> preached the theory that "men of genius decide every-
> thing" and treated revolutionary leaders as omniscient
> and omnipotent deities, whose every word is truth and
> must forever be obeyed. They denied that it is the
> people who make history... According to Lenin, the
> leadership of a proletarian party usually consists of
> people recognized as leaders. Leaders are not gods.
> **They are not infallible and therefore they should not
> be deified.** (<u>BR</u>,10/5:33, 15, 17, 21)

It is perhaps interesting to remark at this point that the Chinese word for "genius" is tianzai天才, a word of Confucian origin that literally means "divine talent."

The above criticism, and the very words in which it here appears, are far from new. In fact, it dates, almost verbatim, from official communiques which appeared in October 1976 at the time of the arrest of the Gang of Four. Foreign Maoists in leadership positions have not misread its implications. Thus Charles Bettelheim, president of the Franco-Chinese Friendship Association, in his letter of resignation, dated May 11, 1977, bluntly remarks:

> The way in which the "criticism" of the Four has been and is being conducted has nothing in common with Chairman Mao's teachings. There is no Marxist analysis to be found in the published material, simply slander and scandal, the low level indicating the inability of the present Chinese Communist Party leadership to develop any serious criticism of what the Four's political line might have been. (Burton:10)

Bettelheim understandably calls the present situation in China "a giant leap backwards." He was not the only one to be baffled. Even now, the difficulty of adjusting to the present line of thinking is still very real, and may remain so until the fate of the Gang of Four is sealed by the courts

Recent publications prove this much: Mao can be shown as being very anti-Mao; Mao can be used to bury Mao. One dazibao described him as having been "30% good and 70% bad." Meanwhile Deng Xiaoping pleaded for calm and recalls that Mao himself has said that the Cultural Revolution was "30% bad and 70% good." Herewith Deng set the tone and indicated the permissible volume of Mao-criticism. Since March there has been a growing crackdown on dissidents. The new emphasis is on "the rule of law." This is so as much to enforce conformity as to protect the individual. There are as yet no major relaxations in the realm of human rights.

Hence it is safe to conclude that, at least for some time, Mao will continue to testify for and against Mao. The pending trial of the Gang of Four might become definitive for Mao's position in PRC history. Meanwhile we can only conjecture and ask ourselves whether Mao is dead, or whether he is still very much alive. Perhaps at the thought of a Red Guards slogan which he inspired, his corpse is shuddering in the splendor of his mausoleum: "He who does not fear being quartered dares throw the emperor off his horse."

Chapter 3:

The quality of Chinese life

"We are a poor and backward nation," Deng keeps telling his foreign visitors. And he must be taken literally. China's poverty, nevertheless, is a poverty with dignity, and the general quality of her people's lives marks a definite improvement over the past. But China remains a vast country in which natural disasters such as floods, droughts and earthquakes are endemic, and hence, there is also sporadic starvation.

To understand the present situation in correct perspective it is good to recall that, in 1927-29 alone, 2.5-million people died of starvation in Shanxi province. This means one-third of the then population. It is estimated that, during the 19th century, 100-million Chinese died of hunger. All admirable progress notwithstanding, it should then not come as a total surprise that, according to a June declaration of Chairman Hua, close to 100-million Chinese live on the level of minimum subsistence. While Hua gave no details, it is a good guess that most of these semi-starving people are, as in the past, China's peasants.

1. The problem of malnutrition

There are at least 800-million peasants in China. It is for their sake, and with their support, that Mao launched his revolution. On the basis of Hua's and other declarations the question has been asked: Does hunger in China point to the failure of a system? (Worldview, 10:44-49)

One is shocked to learn from the People's Daily (PD, 11, 26, 1978, that "in many areas the production level and living standard of the masses at present are lower than those of pre-liberation days or the time of war against Japan." Reference is here to the once fertile Huangtu Plateau, an area of 200,000 square kilometers spread across six northwestern provinces. "Huangtu" means loess soil.

On March 20, the New China News Agency also known as
Xinhua, a semi-official organization, reported that land in
the huangtu region is still "blindly reclaimed" and farmed
to very low yields. "The poorer one becomes, the more land
one reclaims, and the more land one reclaims, the poorer
one becomes."

We also know through the official media that the 1977-8
drought plagued fourteen provinces well into 1979. Last
winter there was famine in Inner Mongolia. On January 26,
there was an appeal over radio for "relief work," as well
as for "self-support," a code word for insufficient assistance by the government. A "comfort group" visited the
stricken land north of the Great Wall, a clear indication
that a major disaster had occurred. Highranking cadre members distributed "some grain, meat, cotton cloth and coal"
and encouraged people "to solve difficulties with their own
efforts." Similar reports came in from other areas such as
Hubei and Yunnan. The Ming Pao of 1/19, published in Hong
Kong, has this distressing news from Sichuan, one of China's
grain producing provinces in the South:

> In 1976 there was harvest failure and the peasants had
> not enough food with which to moisten their mouths. A
> great number of girls were sold to Heilongjiang for a
> price of US$400.00 worth of grain coupons. These
> coupons could be mailed back to Sichuan to support the
> parents. Northern Heilongjiang is a place of em-
> ployment for ex-convicts who have completed their pri-
> son terms. Many of them are single and so these girls
> became their wives.

Earlier I mentioned how shocked I felt at the sight of
women and children being sold in Tianjin, victims of hunger.
The Beijing-connected Hong Kong monthly Tongxiang, in its
May issue, writes that "during the Cultural Revolution, the
incidence of buying and selling brides rose abnormally."
Related to this matter, one avowal coming from high places
must suffice. Says Ms. Kang Keqing, Chairperson of the National Women's Union:

> Over the last decade or more ... not only has our nation's
> economy come to the brink of collapse, but social moral-
> ity was also greatly corrupted, to such an extent that
> there was restoration of the buying and selling of brides
> or of such practice in disguise... In our country there
> is a great difference between the city and relatively
> poor villages... In places where production levels and
> living standards are low, the buying and selling of
> brides are not easy to eliminate completely. (PD, 12/27,
> 1978)

During the last several months, the Chinese press continues to report on the falsification of agricultural statistics to the detriment of the farmers. We have also been given accurate descriptions of techniques used to deceive the government as well. Thus a long essay in the PD of April 20 complains that in many places "statistics continue to serve politics and do not reflect economic reality." On May 7, the same newspaper remarks that "30 per cent is statistics, 70 per cent is guesswork."

There are no doubt serious efforts towards an equitable distribution of food. But inadequate storage, processing, and transport enormously complicate this task. Lack of refrigeration accounts for the fact that large quantities of fish rot before they reach port. To quote the PD of January 2: "In summer and winter, fresh fish spoils within an hour or two and thus must be dumped back into the sea."

There is one bright side to all this dismal news: the misery of the peasants is now publicly admitted. Official voices have called for an end to "indiscriminate requisition and the harassment of peasants." (PD, 1/24) Redress will not be easy. People in local authority remain "afraid of the wolf in front and the tiger behind." The top leadership is aware that the Chinese peasantry feel deprived and are vengeful. Already authority within the three-tiered structure of the communes (commune, production brigade, production team) is breaking down in favor of the right of self-determination. The government assures the peasants that better times will come, but that they cannot be realized at once.

Fortunately China's peasant masses muster an impressive dose of patience, an unfailing energy, and a capacity for human survival perhaps unmatched by any other nation in the world. We must not forget that China tries to feed 23% of the world's population; that she imports 7-8% of all the wheat, and exports 10 to 20% of all the rice, that moves in global trade.

Developing (and other) nations have much to learn from China, such as labor-intensive cropping, low-technology methods, and the use of fertilizers. China has an exemplary system of agricultural education. Its cottage industries keep people employed in rural areas and away from the cities. Communes are a system of management, and a "collective capitalism" adapted to Chinese peasant life.

In fact, already China helps the world through an exchange of information on seed varieties and labor-intensive farming methods. China spreads out its influence in global food and agricultural organizations. It stands therefore to reason, as Charles P. Lutz writes in <u>Lutheran World Federation News Service</u>, 11/13, that "The world's food security can only be increased as its largest nation takes a more active part in the international councils for planning, information-sharing and agreement-writing." Lutz is an expert. He is also coordinator of the American Lutheran Church's hunger program and he reports on an October visit to agricultural areas in China.

Mao's dictum that "China's future are her peasants" raises the question of balance between the four modernizations -- industry, technology, army, and agriculture. Already industrial growth outpaces agricultural development with the result that there is a widening gap between standards of living in rural and in urban communities. This may well spell disaster and trigger a new revolution, particularly after thousands of foreign-trained students return home without any experience of village life. The West dare not forget that Mao never went abroad; that he kept in touch with the masses, and that he vigorously opposed the thought of a privileged elite sitting on top of eight hundred million peasants clamoring for food and human dignity.

BASIC NECESSITIES ARE IMPORTANT

As we were walking, I noticed an older woman walking in the street. She was carying a brown paper bag. Suddenly, someone jostled her and the bag ripped. Out came rice grains. She proceeded to sit down in the street, surrounded by passing bikes and people, and pick up every grain of rice. I couldn't help but think that in Hong Kong, we would simply get a broom and sweep it down the sewer. The woman had the strangest look, so resigned to things and like a woman with a terrific burden. (<u>Mission Forum</u>:46)

---

2. The new economy

It is not true, as guides tell their visitors, that the Gang of Four is responsible for a decade's stagnation of Chinese economy. From 1949, when Mao came to power, until 1975 on the even of his death, China's growth rate of national output ranged among the four highest of 100 developing countries. Mao never sacrificed economic development on the altar of ideology -- nor, I submit, will his successors, Hua and Deng. Thus "self-reliance" and a host of other proven Maoist virtues have not been abandoned as Bettelheim would claim. "Self-reliance" then and now means "keeping the initiative in one's hands." And this proud policy remains unchanged.

But if goals remain the same in China, methods do change. In Deng's words, "There must be less empty talk and more hard work!" The government is conscious of the fact that nothing stimulates hard work as much as free enterprise. According to official reports, free enterprise is now making a quiet come-back under the new code name of "collectively owned shops and small industries." This turn-over is as unobtrusive as it is irreversible. During the last few months, the quantity of goods and the quality of service, particularly in the cities, have much improved. The erstwhile bourgeois slogan "Profit before politics" now reads in two new versions: "Profit for politics" and "Politics for profit."

Incentives, the government discovered, make for good business. They also provide new jobs in a country which acutely feels the pinch of unemployment, although not yet to the extent of the West. Thus the Beijing Review, 10/19, enthusiastically reports that, according to official statistics, "4.48-million young people had been provided with jobs by the end of August."

Of these, 2.35-million are city-bred youth waiting for employment, and 1.74-million are young people who returned from the countryside to the cities. The rest are college or secondary and vocational school graduates and demobilized soldiers. Among the newly employed, 3.33-million of 74.5% of the total, have been assigned to collectively owned enterprises which employ large numbers of people, need very little investment, and are responsible for their own profits and losses, thus entailing no state expenditures for the wages of the newly employed.

The above statistics are interesting if vague. Perhaps

they imply that 25.5% of the new August work force "were
assigned" to private enterprises, a fact which would under-
line the vastness of economic change in China.

The concomitant effects of a partial return to free enterprise were felt almost immediately. The leadership in
Beijing raised retail prices of major food items, including
beef, pork, mutton, seafood, eggs, poultry and milk (but
not rice or vegetables) by about 33%, an increase which
would affect urbanites more than peasants whose income has
been rising with the grain crops of this summer.

In what is described as "the boldest move in a progres-
sive policy on income since the rise to power of Senior
Vice-premier Deng Xiaoping," the government lifted price
controls from more than 10.000 products -- or about one-
fifth of all commodities on sale in China. Such a thing
had not happened since 1957. To accommodate urban workers,
it was also decided to raise their salaries by US$3.3 per
month. About 40% of these workers would get pay rises over
and above their salaries "on the basis of merit, taking
into consideration work contributions, attitude towards
work and technical level achieved." (Asiaweek, 11/16; BR,
11/9:4)

The first inkling of a prices revolution came from Vice-
premier Li Xiennien in his address to the Fifth National
People's Congress in May. Li put it somewhat bluntly: "If
you do more, you get more; if you don't work at all, you
get nothing. We think only by so doing can we possibly
fire the enthusiasm of the workers." At these words, audi-
ble cries of anger and dismay went up from foreign orthodox Maoist circles. Chairman Mao, they said, believed that
only "spiritual incentives" were appropriate, and that
"material incentives" were unseemly in a communist state.
If they had been better informed, they might have known
that "material incentives" dominated the industrial scene
under Mao as much as now. After all, it is good Marxist
theory that, in the socialist stage (the one which precedes
the communist stage), income is distributed according to
work, a fact of which Vice-premier Li has reminded us.
Mao's successors are therefore quite orthodox, and, of all
people, Mr Deng, the de facto leader of China, should
know. He paid heavily in his person (he was sent off to
work in a canteen) and in his daughter's person (she was
maimed by the Red Guards) for advocating "material incentives." While little has changed in fact, Mr Deng perhaps
now savors his sweet revenge as the Gang of Four prepare
for trial.

3. The control of population

Together with political stability and the financing of the Four Modernizations, the rapid increase of population is the gravest problem China is obliged to face. We now have, for the first time, official statistics, released by the State Statistical Bureau on December 28, which put China's population at over 1-billion. The increase can be measured if compared with previous statistics, published by the same agency, last June when the population stood at 975.230-million. The one before this last census came out twenty-five years ago. It then put the population at 580-million. At the recent rate of increase, China's population would reach unmanageable dimensions in the years to come. Hence the alarm in the press, and a flood of official directives which set as the nation's goal "to have couples limit their children to only one, so that, by the year 2000, the population will hit the zero mark."

These are words from the pen of Vice-premier Chen Muhua found at the end of an instructive article in which she discusses the significance of bringing population growth under control, "in a planned way, and in relation to the Four Modernizations." Chen's full text is found in the BR, 11/16, to which I'm mostly indebted for what follows.

In her opening statement, Ms. Chen admits that, "because we failed to understand this problem years ago, our population has been multiplying uncontrolled." Allow me to remark that it would have been more accurate for Ms. Chen to say that, also in the recent past, population control was attempted, and particularly since 1954. But, then as much as now, it met with considerable opposition and largely failed. For the interested reader, details on this matter may be found in an article by Han Su-yin, the well-known pro-communist writer, in The New York Times, 7/1, 1973; in Peyrefitte: 280-4, and, very recently, in de Villiers: 328-30.

But back to Ms. Chen. On the way to zero growth, there are two stages, the first stage consists in "aiming to reduce the growth rate of 12 per thousand to about 5 per thousand in 1985... This is a herculean task."

We expect that by 1985 no one will have a third child, which means there will be five million babies fewer each year and a drop in the population growth rate of 7 per thousand or less... The main way to attain zero population growth is to energetically encourage each couple to have only one child.

In fact, we are told, already in Beijing's Haidian District, a suburban area with a huge rural population, about 30% of all women want only one child. "To encourage people to have only one child, a series of social and economic measures will be adopted and enforced." Among these measures: material awards, such as an increase in subsidies and old age pensions, housing and health priorities. "Single-child parents, if necessary, can stay home to look after a sick child without having their pay docked." There are specific deterrents for large families: "Parents insisting on having many children have their bonuses cut. Those who insist having more than two children have to pay the state or the collective a monthly sum amounting to 10% of their wages."

Strenuous efforts will be made "to solve people's ideological as well as practical problems." It is admitted that some old concepts stand in the way, such as "the greatest filial piety is to have a male offspring," or "the more sons, the better," or also, "a son is better than a daughter," and "raise sons to provide for one's old age." All these "olds" are still very much alive. Some people even quote Mao's well-known dictum: "One mouth is two arms." But, the PRC leadership feels, all this can be overcome through strong persuasion, and by an appeal to the noblest patriotic feelings of the people.

By way of example, Han Su-yin tells of the following case:

One woman got pregnant inadvertently and out of turn; she was thus taking away the possibility of giving birth from another woman who had no baby and wanted to give birth. (All women in that commune had pledged not to have more than two children.) This woman not to interfere with her neighbor, then had an abortion, although she had only two girls and wanted a boy. It was public-spirited of her.

Visitors to Shanghai report finding an array of contraceptives much in public view, the latest addition being a pill for men called Gossypol. (der überblick: 21-2) David Perlman was told that this arrangement worked quite well: "It led to a threefold increase in the contraceptives distributed, as people are no longer embarrassed to ask." The prescribed marriage age for girls is 25; for boys it is 25 in the countryside and 27 in the cities. (BR, 11/30:6) Permission to marry must be obtained. "When girls under 23 ask for contraceptives," a pharmacist told Perlman, "we ask them for identification if they seem too young. But we will give them the pill anyway because it is better to use contraceptives then to become pregnant. Still, such people will be taught the correct behavior by the comrades in their neighborhood or work place." (SFC, 10/2)

It is difficult for anyone who has not bodily felt the crush of people in China's larger cities to understand the poignancy in the matter of population control which confronts the Chinese masses. In Beijing one sees children forced to attend classes under the trees because there are not enough classrooms. Ms. Chen tells us that "6% of the children reaching school age cannot go to school; 12% of the children having finished primary school cannot continue their studies... Only about 5% of the senior middle school graduates have a chance to get a college education. Alongside this problem is the difficulty of finding employment."

Shopping for food in the crowded cities is an all-day ordeal. The Gongren Ribao (Workers' Daily), in a front-page report, November 13, has a worker complain: "If we have any spare time, we are so busy eating, drinking, and attending to household duties, that we go through the whole day with aching heads. How can we possibly have the strength to think of the Four Modernizations, or carry them out?" This man lives in Beijing's Chaoyang district with a population of more than 800.000 people and 500 factories. There are only two small cinemas and one workers' club in that neighborhood.

Problems in Shanghai are similar to those in Beijing. In principle, newlyweds are entitled to leave their parents and move into new quarters with at least 12 square meters of living space. (In older buildings, families are allocated housing on the basis of four square meters per adult.) Rent is a nominal seven yuan (less than five dollars) per month in new buildings with gas, electricity, and cold water but no heat of hot water. Even so, couples must wait months and sometimes years for new housing.

Although unemployed educated youth are the particular legacy of the Cultural Revolution, Shanghai has been trying to disperse its population since the early days of the People's Republic. From 1950 to 1972, more than 1.5-million people have been moved out of Shanghai to remote and border provinces. Before the Cultural Revolution, the dispersal policy was relatively lenient. But from 1966, when the Cultural Revolution began, 100% of high school graduates were sent to the countryside -- 940,000 altogether to provinces, such as Heilongjiang in the north, Yunnan in the south, as well as closer areas such as Anhui or Jiangsu. The 100% policy was wrong. Nevertheless, only 300,000 of the 940,000 have so far been permitted to return. (CSM, 12/28)

In every country, lack of schooling and lack of work leads youth to crime. The Chinese press admits that "a wave of crime haunts city streets." (Time, 12/10) The Liberation

Daily reports that young girls are afraid to venture out of their homes and that "some criminals have been publicly blocking roads, committing robberies, murders, rapes, and thefts of both public and private property." On December 5, Deng Xiaoping, receiving an Encyclopoedia Britannica delegation defended the stiff 15-year sentence meted out in October to Wei Jingsheng on the ground that "we needed to make an example of him." Other leaders, however, felt differently and took pity on the man.

Population control involves more than persuasion; it also means human suffering. The whole world waits to see the effects of China's new policy upon the wellbeing and happiness of her people.

FOR THE PERSON WHO HAS NOT SHARED IN THE CHINESE EXPERIENCE itself -- not even from the outside, so to speak, Marxist ideology, itself originally of western inspiration and containing influences derived from both the Jewish and Christian traditions, can appear the convenient gateway to an understanding of China. One may then overlook all that is uniquely Chinese in Chinese Communism, as one tends to do in the continuum of the entire Chinese historical experience. It is possible then to run the risk of seeing in Marxism a means of interpreting once and for all the Chinese experience, and end up understanding nothing at all, not even oneself. And this, tragically enough, has been the mistake of generations of missionaries who sought only to understand China through Christian ideas of sin and grace, of salvation and conversion and damnation.

Julia Ching in Chu, p. 21

Chapter 4:

The Fifth Modernization: Democracy and Human Rights

Since the overthrow of the hated Gang of Four in 1976, China's new gospel is that of the Four Modernizations. Friendly critics of the regime, domestic as well as foreign, are wondering whether, apart from the modernization of agriculture, industry, science and technology, and defense, there is not, and should not be, an equal call for a fifth modernization, that of democracy and human rights, without which, they fear, the four other modernizations are bound to fail. Obviously, this is the thesis defended by many of the Big Character Posters at Democracy Wall.

It is somewhat more surprising to find the same thesis advocated by semi-official spokespersons, such as historian Li Shu who recently gave a report on "Thirty Years of China's Social Sciences" in which he reviews "the zigzag process of history." Li concludes with these significant words:

> To promote social sciences, we must give full play to democracy, and call for scientific study of the policies, theories and practical problems of socialist construction. Full freedom should be given to such research and to discussions of its findings. Science will flourish if a democractic system is guaranteed and if it is encouraged and not restricted. Only when science advances and the cultural level of the people rises, can China's socialist modernization develop at high speed. (BR, 12/21:30)

Official reactions to the posters, and to the spirit which they evoke, show the depth of the dilemma in which the leadership finds itself. Earlier I have mentioned Vice-premier Deng's statement to the effect that "We needed to make an example of Mr Wei." Deng's words have called forth a variety of reactions:

Some are concerned at the apparent use of the Wei trial as a warning to others not to overstep the bounds
of permissible criticism. If this is so, how meaning-
ful, they ask, is the new criminal law passed by the
National People's Congress in July, providing that the
right of the person, democratic rights, and other
rights of citizens shall be protected against unlawful
infringement by any person or institution? (CSM, 11/9)

It would appear on the face of official statements that
the Chinese masses are craving for law in protection
against a repeat performance by any new Gang of Four. It
would not come as a surprise if this feeling were strongly
shared by many of the present leaders, and particularly by
Deng Xiaoping, one of the outstanding victims of the Cultural Revolution.

Mr Deng has given ample proof that he is fully aware of
the need to involve the masses in his projects of modernization. However, with many other leaders, Deng may fear
that the recent unleashing of criticism, and the instant
demand for higher standards of living need reining in lest
they jeopardize the pace of progress since he came to power.
Be that as it may, the restoration of human rights to a
mass of people unjustly condemned, imprisoned and sometimes
tortured during the fifties and later is now seriously attempted. While thousands still await rehabilitation, a
single directive of the Central Committee in the spring of
1977, ordered the release of 110.000 people who had lost
their freedom and possessions in the crisis of 1957. (CN,
Spring 1978:24)

It is unlikely that, in distant provinces, young people
could have read what April Fifth Forum, the voice of a
dissident group, recently wrote: "The development of science requires a definite kind of soil, and that soil is democracy." Yet, if we must believe a Radio Beijing broadcast
of December 3, the situation in some of these places may be
somewhat tense: "Some 1500 soldiers were sent out to 800
schools to suppress the anarchism and individualism that
lives among the students. The soldiers have orders to
inspire the students with respect for law and public morality." (De Standaard, 12/6)

The stationing of troops at schools and universities is
nothing new. A recent case in point is reported by the
BR, 10/19, from which I quote:

Students of the People's University in Beijing resumed
classes three days after they went on strike... The
University was forced to close down during the Cultural
Revolution and its campus was turned over to the People's Liberation Army. With the increase in the enrol-
ment in this term, however, the shortage of buildings
became acute. Though the university authorities appealed repeatedly to the Army, the question was not
solved which led to the suspension of classes on October 10. A settlement was reached on October 12 with
the assistance of higher authorities. Within a fixed
date, the Army would release some buildings. The stu-
dent council called on the students to study hard and
to strengthen unity with the Army.

Visitors to China are enthusiastic about the openness
with which students talk to them; about the high quality
of their English and other foreign languages, and about
their desire to know more about the outside world. Moreover, thousands of students are being prepared for studies
abroad. A first group of seventy arrived in Paris on January 25. The cultural attaché at the Chinese Embassy reminded them upon arrival that, fifty years earlier, Chinese had come to France "to study, and to prepare for making China become a free and powerful nation." And among
their predecessors, the attaché mentioned by name of Zhou
Enlai and Deng Xiaoping. The students then went to the
Notre Dame Cathedral. They were amazed to see so few bicycles and so many traffic jams...

At this writing, some sixty Chinese students are in Belgium. Vice-rector Servotte told me that "these Chinese
students already speak Flemish better than some of our
compatriots." One of the students has asked for asylum.
Once more, the sending of students abroad is not a break
with the past. During the 1950s, 38.000 Chinese went to
Russia for advanced training.

Will educational reforms in China lead to a democratization of the country? We do not know. Whatever the answer,
such a democratization will be, and ought to be, a statecraft congenial to the Chinese genius. In a remarkable article by Wu Jialin, we read this comparison between two
types of democracy:

Socialist democracy is superior to bourgeois democracy. This is determined by the nature of the socialist system. Our socialist system determines that
our socialist democracy should and can be superior to
bourgeois democracy. But, "should be" does not mean
"actually is" and "can" does not denote "in reality."

It is, to say the least, a naive illusion to think
that the system of a socialist democracy arises and
becomes complete of its own accord without a long
period of practice and hard struggle.

Democracy and human rights, most Chinese would agree,
are the inseparable twin pillars of a humane society. We
have been put on notice by the Chinese representative
in a speech at the General Assembly of the United Nations,
October 23, how human rights are seen by his government:

> We think that a certain legal framework under which
> human rights are guaranteed is always necessary. In
> the legislation of many countries, individual rights
> are often embodied in the form of rights of citizens.
> Since the social system and actual condition vary from
> state to state, the legal provisions on the rights of
> citizens are bound to be different. This is the inter-
> nal affair of each state and brooks no interference by
> outsiders. (BR,11/2)

A week later, in its issue of November 9, Beijing Review
published extensive excerpts from an article in Guangming
Ribao, a respected organ of the Communist press. The topic:
human rights in a socialist society. Some statements in
that article throw an interesting light upon the official
attitude toward religion in China. Hence this long quotation:

> Compared with those in capitalist countries, human
> rights in a socialist country with a different social
> system have at least two fundamental characteristics.
> One is that, in capitalist countries, the sacredness
> and inviolability of private property are the most
> basic rights of citizens, while the Chinese Constitution
> stipulates that "socialist public property shall be
> inviolable" and "citizens must take care of and protect
> public property." The other is that citizens' rights
> in China are actual and not nominal or hypocritical for
> every citizen... Only those targets of the dictatorship
> -- the hostile elements, the counter-revolutionaries
> and other criminals who make up a very small minority
> of the population -- are deprived of their political
> rights (part of citizens' rights) for a definite period
> according to law.

> When we say that the socialist system fundamentally
> ensures that every citizen actually enjoys all the
> rights according to law, we do not mean that under
> socialist conditions, people can naturally, fully and
> without hindrance enjoy all citizens' rights. The
> socialist superstructure is not yet perfect, bureau-
> cratism still exists, there are defects in some links

of our state system and the legal system is not yet complete, -- all explain why sometimes the people have no reliable guarantee for their democratic rights, freedom of the person, and legitimate economic rights and interests... All rights are restricted by certain material conditions and cultural levels, ... in the absence of which the citizen cannot fully enjoy the different kinds of rights.

Piecing together recent official statements on people "set free" and "rehabilitated," it is evident that the number of those who were unjustly deprived of their rights runs into the millions. Small wonder then that, some observers feel, Gulags do exist in China.

. China's largest province, Qinghai, is a forbidding, windswept high plateau of 280.000 square miles. Daniel Kelly, an American prisoner who spent two and a half years there told _Time_, November 28, that Qinghai is literally a prison colony. Of the 4-million population, half are either prisoners or forced laborers. All are forbidden to leave their prison without bars. Perhaps only one out of one hundred Qinghai prisoners ever leaves the province alive. There is no physical torture, only hard work, starvation and the systematic crushing of the human spirit. It is surmised that there are hundreds of prison camps, or rather "labor camps" throughout the country. Many Catholics, priests and bishops, who were condemned to long prison terms have recently been "set free" only to exchange one prison system for another. They remain silent witnesses to the fact that "sometimes the people have no guarantee for their democratic rights."

Of course, this is only one aspect of the Chinese reality. But it is an important aspect which needed to be mentioned, particularly at the hand of Chinese sources. At the same time, I suggest, one should also recognize that, during the last thirty   years, China's institutions have produced more social and economic progress and more equality than in many other countries of the world. There is much to learn from China, also in the matter of democracy and human rights. But the question remains: Progress at what price of human suffering?

Chapter 5:

The limits of westernization

_____

    From all I have said, the problem facing China is fairly
clear: What path ought and could she travel to reach a
classless, cohesive, highly productive, agricultural and
industrial, free and Maoist, society? The Great Helmsman
had an answer, however tentative, and perhaps now on the
point of being abandoned. He advocated a yin-yang type of
alternating periods of rapid revolutionary progress followed by spells of moderation; of first letting loose, later
to pull in the reins; of letting bloom a hundred flowers,
later to cut off their unwanted shoots. All this he learned from Marx and Lenin. All this Hua and Deng learned from
Mao. As there is no straight and true path to Communism,
at the exclusion of all other paths, so there is no single
straight and true path to present-day Chinese policy, be
it in the matter of economy, human rights or religion.

    This does not imply that many achievements of the Chin-
ese leadership do not deserve our admiration. I for one
would emphatically want to support all efforts of the
Chinese people to reach the best socialist society which
they can get. And I strongly believe their leaders when
they say that "the best" still remains to be worked out,
both in theory and in practice.

    Hence, I find no justification for the fashionable in-
terpretation, particularly rampant in America since January, 1979, "the hour of normalization," to the effect that
Mao is an impractical ideologist, and Deng a hardheaded
realist. The means they use may differ, but the goal they
covet remains the same. History may argue that, in applying their means, and in setting their goals, both Mao and
Deng drove too hastily and reached out too far. For Mao,
the Greap Leap Forward in 1958-9, and later the Cultural
Revolution, dismally backfired and cost the fall of many.

Could the same happen to Deng? What then are the limits
of that "westernization" (to use a very unsatisfactory
word) which he has energetically touched off? I venture
the guess that Deng is a fairly good prophet, and I believe
him when he tells us that China will be one of the most
powerful countries by the end of this century. But whether
it will be Maoist, or even socialist, at that time, I
submit with due modesty, not even Deng could know.

We have interesting information on the limits of wester-
nization in an interview which Premier Hua gave to Felix
Greene, Vice-president of the Society for Anglo-Chinese
Understanding, on September 11, from which I quote:

Greene: Don't you think that "modernization" might
lead to a kind of "westernization" of China, with all
the problems involved? For example, machines replace
workers -- so won't this only increase your problem of
unemployment?

Hua: I think you may have notices that China's modernization program rests on two premises. The first is
to achieve modernization on the foundation of a socialist system. The second is that it must be carried
out in the light of conditions in China and done in a
Chinese way... There are no grounds for thinking that
it will inevitably lead to "westernization" or bring
us back to capitalism. Our accepting foreign invest-
ments and increasing economic and cultural exchanges
with other countries may, of course, be accompanied
by the spread of some western influences. This is
something to wath out for. We believe that our people
can tell the good from the bad and will resist and
overcome bad influences... I hope my visit to Western
Europe will help deepen understanding and friendship
between the Chinese people, the French people, the
people in West Germany, the British people and the
Italian people, open up broader prospects for amicable
cooperation and contribute to the maintenance of world
peace. (BR, 10/19)

Will China become America-in-the-Orient and the model of
a socialist-consumerist society by the year 2000? Most probably not. There is, of course, no lack of pleasant little
innovations which titillate the foreign press. Coca-cola
is "in," but it is still a bit suspect for its "bourgeois"
taste, and, in tourist places, it must be bought with foreign currency. Until a few years ago, the old big four
treasures were a bicycle, a wristwatch, a sewing machine,
and a radio. Now these four are so widely available that
they no longer serve as status symbols or bring prestige.

The New China News Agency, on January 1, 1980, formally announced the arrival of a "new big four": a television set at the top of the heap, closely followed by a tape recorder, electric fan, and a washing machine. In fact, 35% of families in the Beijing city area have television sets. As for the "old big four," they are as common as chopsticks in a restaurant. Statistics show that for every 100 families there are now 62 sewing machines, 144 bicycles, 100 transistor radios, and 222 wristwatches...

Equally important is a change in staple foods: people eat more bread, and soon they may have instant rice, mass-produced noodles, packaged dinners, and, God forbid, Big Macs. We are told that "the government encourages farmers to raise chickens instead of forbidding them to do so as was the practice previously." In fact, chickens are a very precious commodity in rural China. "There is a new small radio on the market which sells for the price of four hens and is very popular with the farmers." (BR, 10/26:4; 12/7:6)

The government has launched a successful non-smoking drive with films, medicinal candy which makes smoking unpleasant and a huge billboard in Wangfujing, Beijing's busy shopping center. "A single drop of nicotine is enough to kill three horses," declares one sign. (BR, 12/14:29)

In November, Herbert von Karajan charmed his Beijing audiences, and startled Chinese journalists with his misogynist remark: "No women in the Berlin Philharmonic!" After von Karajan came Yehudi Menuhin who brought down the house, not only with his virtuoso playing but even more so with his parting words: "From what I have already heard here, I feel that we in the West have as much to learn as to give." (BR, 12/21:31) This is quite true, and not only in the field of music.

CHRIST'S SUFFERING, CHINA'S SUFFERING

The passio Christi apud Sinenses must be taken in its full range. Calvary in China covers not only the heroic dead of the Communist Liberation Army, but also the victims of Nanking, Kuomintang casualties, prisoners in labor camps, and all those professionals and academics who have seen their disciplines suppressed after the Communist Revolution.

Gerald O'Collins, S.J., in Chu, p. 133

A few years ago, Peyrefitte could write: "La Chine se veut un couvent." This is no longer the case; China has lost her monkish smell. Coquetry is back, and de Villiers tells us that "love is rehabilitated." (p. 250) In Shanghai, thousands line up to see Gina Lollobrigida on the magic screen. In Beijing, western ballet is a must for visiting dignitaries and ordinary workers. Some even claim that it honorably competes with the Bolshoi. In the PRC, success does not always spoil the heart. After a brilliant performance, a friend of mine recently was allowed to go backstage and congratulate the prima ballerina. Somewhat inadvertedly he asked about her salary. She shot back at him: "Sir, you are insulting me. Why should I be paid more than an ordinary worker just for the sake of these legs?"

China has asked UNESCO to help finance her foreign language program to the tune of $15-million. The aid would be used to   train technicians in English, French, German, Japanese and other languages so they can go abroad for study. China is also seeking aid from the World Health Organization in setting up medical training centers. At the United Nations, Chinese argue their positions with great sophistication. They now take an interest in such issues as disarmament and the North-South dialogue which, until recently they had declared to be "pseudo-problems." China now methodically courts the United States which represents half of the "first world" according to Mao's categorization. The PRC also turns to the "second world" which is Japan and Western Europa. With all these countries China has signed important economic and often cultural agreements.

Few capitalists remain in China, and their lot has vastly improved during the last several months:

> High salaries for the capitalists, too, are part of the policy of buying them out. In the past, we paid them high salaries to facilitate their remolding; today, it is better not to reduce the sum in the light of historical factors. According to preliminary estimates,   there are only about 800 former capitalists in the country who receive a monthly salary of over 300 yuan. Most of these are representatives or technical and managerial personnel of the former national bourgeoisie. Their high pay accounts for only a very small fraction of the state's wage expenditure. (BR, 11/16:13)

On Sunday, November 25, the first exhibition of modern art opened its doors in Beijing and drew 2000 people. Reactions to this western style artistic display were mixed. Some visitors applauded the victory of twenty-three "rebel artists" over the Gang of Four's oppression. Others looked sincerely nonplussed at the imaginative daring and the exotic features of an array of drawings which ranged from pop to nude.

The list of pleasant _faits divers_ pointing to some little twist toward "westernization" gets longer every day. Unfortunately, we have no proven hermeneutics to help us read the future.

On December 8, my radio tells me that the Democracy Wall is already a monument to the past. Pity poor Han Su-yin, China's self-appointed prophetess who, only ten years ago, wrote in her China in the Year 2001, Penguin Books, 1970, p. 192, that "big-character posters have given so much astonishment in the West, yet they are merely the free expression of public opinion, and as such the most obvious feature of the practice of democracy being taught today."

But I stand by Ms Han when she says at the end of her book that "the remaking of man is being attempted for one quarter of mankind" in China. She is quite convincing when she adds: "The process of the humanization of man is the one which resists brutality and animality, depersonalization and the return to barbarism." She goes on to quote Chairman Mao on the destiny of the Chinese people as "bringing a much greater contribution to humanity... than they have so far."

My heart tells me that this is true, for which I give thanks to God. And my faith tells me that this dream will not turn into reality until the day when China and the Church look one another straight in the eyes -- and like what they see.

TRENDS: TWO CUTS FROM THE BEIJING REVIEW

"A single drop of
nicotine is enough
to kill three horses."

The latest pattern. Paper-cut by Zhao Yuliang

Chapter 6:

The Chinese people view their own achievements

I have so far convered only a few aspects of Chinese
life. In no way do I intend to sound critical of China's
real achievements in which millions justly take pride,
and I invite the reader to have an attentive look at the
most recent Christian literature on this subject to cross
my desk: a special issue of der überblick, December 1979,
on "China, development country."

Employment is the key to social security. China has no
Ministry of Labor, but instead it disposes of a vast net-
work of "labor bureaus" which, since July 1979, directly
control the labor force, particularly incoming youths.
Through advanced and long-range planning, it is hoped to
find 7.5-million new jobs during 1979, which is almost
double the quota reached in 1978.

Chinese communists glorify labor as an honor; it is their
gateway to promotion and a university education. Labor
identifies the person with the masses. Only a proletarian
is entitled to join the ruling class. Hence, all must participate in production as a means to acquire a spirit of
"service to the masses." Even though at present more and
more exceptions are permitted, the ideal remains for university professors, civil servants, artists and writers,
to spend three to six months every two or three years
on farms or in factories. A Beijing scientist told a
friend of mine: "In the West, you have your sabbatical
year, and you like it. I wouldn't want to miss my work in
a factory or on a farm. I want to be with the people."

Since 1977, students have requested more courses in
Chinese literature. At the end of that year, for the
first time since the Cultural Revolution, collections of
classical Chinese poetry appeared on the market, along
with reissues of Shakespeare, Victor Hugo, Tolstoy,
Goethe, Cervantes and Dante. It was reported that a line
a hundred yards long formed at a Beijing bookstore to
buy the first copies of Hamlet. In March 1978, a 3-volume

collection of Einstein's works came out, including his
social and political essays. The famous physicist received this encomium from Xinghua, the official news
agency, March 15, 1978:

> It goes without saying that Einstein was not free of
> the faults and limitations of his time. The seeking
> of truth and serving the interests of humanity, how-
> ever, remained a goal throughout his life. The spiri-
> tual fruits of his labor and his strenuous defiance of
> violence can never be eclipsed. He is a giant shining
> star in the history of mankind.

At this writing, most books can freely be sent to China,
although some magazines, such as Etudes, have been returned.
Every day seems to offer to the Chinese masses new opportunities for widening their knowledge of people around the
world. This autumn, "in the park grounds around the Cultural Palace of the Working People, where the towering
cypress trees reach towards the sky, Xinhua Shudian (New
China Bookstore) held a ten-day book fair. Two hundred
forty thousand people thronged the eight makeshift book-
stalls, buying 350.000 yuan's worth of books." (BR, 12/7:30)
The BR runs a regular column on Culture and Science. In
the November 23 issue, we read:

> China is now publishing 1200 journals, magazines and
> periodicals for national distribution, including 900
> on science and technology, 130 on literature and art
> and the rest on social sciences. In addition, 300
> more will come off the press at a later date.

Much has been written about the enhanced status of women
in Chinese society, and about the new laws which assure
them equality in marriage. The same issue of BR describes
the case of Jiao Shuzhi, 21, who won an annulment of her
forced marriage from the son of her factory manager:

> To safeguard their rights sometimes Chinese citizens
> have to fight against people in powerful positions
> who violate state laws and Party discipline. It is
> easier to win success these days because of support
> from the courts and public opinion.

The new Chinese family too has come in for considerable
praise, even in Catholic periodicals. Thus Raymond Vol-
ant, in the French missionary publication Spiritus, December 1979, describes the PRC family as democratic, based on
equality and liberty, and protected against the former
oppressive influences of the clan. Elderly parents usual-
ly live with their children, which fact accounts for an
average of 4,55 persons per family in China, over against
3,1 in France. Old folks who have no family are taken care

of by the community. But such cases are rare. An old person's salary is higher than that of a young worker, which makes him a desirable addition to the household because he handsomely adds his share to the total income. Obedience and love remain the pillars of a child's education, much as in the past. But there is a significant change: basic human feelings are now directed away from kith and kin also to embrace the Party and the people whoever they may be.

I note with joy that, on these and other facets of Chinese life, information, at the beginning of 1980, is both more accurate and abundant. Before long, we should be able to judge with sufficient confidence the degree of humaneness and happiness which is within reach of the Chinese man in the street.

At this point I should like to raise the intriguing question: To what extent have Mao and his successors attempted the sinification of Marxism, and what does their attempt spell for the future of the PRC?

Mao's early disdain for Confucianism is well known. He repeatedly condemned China's great sage, Confucius, as the representative of a slave-owning feudal society. He forbade all teaching of philosophy, except under strict political supervision. Philosophy books were banned or rewritten to conform to the Maoist point of view. In 1972, however, a sudden rehabilitation of Chinese philosophy began, ostensibly to transform Chinese communism through the influence of traditional Chinese thought, but in fact, as it turned out, to eliminate Party purgees, such as Lin Biao, and even Confucius himself. The pi-Lin-pi-Kung campaign is now almost forgotten, at least as far as Confucius is concerned. Instead we are reminded of the advantages for each school of thought to stress its own identity. Through conflict large areas of harmony are discovered, theory is brought closer to the people, and mutual tolerance is fostered. This state of affairs Mao has called "inter-penetration, inter-permeation, inter-dependence, inter-connection or mutual cooperation." (Selected Works, III: 337)

In true Chinese fashion, I feel that we are witnessing at present a convergence, rather than an opposition, of what, at first glance, seem to be irreducible opposites, Marxism and Chinese traditional philosophy and religiosity. The government of China may very well intend the marxification of Chinese thought; but they may equally be interested in the sinification of Marxism. Precisely on this sinification theory Mao makes interesting reading:

For the Chinese communists who are part of the great nation, flesh of its flesh and blood of its blood,

Cartoons

China Reconstructs

中 國 建 設

DECEMBER 1979

"How come you're putting salt on the news-
paper, Comrade?"
"Because this article has no flavor at all!"
Hua Junwu

Two endless flows.
Zhang Fang

Applying the lever principle
(the best help for chairbound
bureaucrats who refuse to go
where the work is).
Li Bingsheng

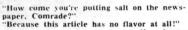

Toy salesman and toy tigers, equally fierce.
Li Shimin and Fan Guanglin

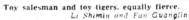

any talk about Marxism in isolation from China's characteristics is merely Marxism in the abstract, Marxism
in a vacuum. Hence, to apply Marxism concretely in
China, so that its every manifestation has an undoubt-
edly Chinese character, i.e., to apply Marxism in the
light of China's specific characteristics, becomes a
problem which is urgent for the whole Party to understand and solve. (Ibid., II:209)

I am impressed by the earnestness with which the Chinese
press, as reflected in the recent issues of the Beijing
Review, treats the whole discussion on Marxism (or rather,
to use the standard term, on Marxism-Leninism-Mao Zedong
Thought) vs. "the Chinese identity." It is generally admitted in ruling circles that Chinese philosophy should be
evaluated chiefly from the standpoint of knowledge, be it
"inborn," as Confucians maintain, or "acquired after birth
through social experience," as Mao would have it. There
is a confrontation here between "idealist apriorism" and
"materialist reflectionism." Only the latter is acceptable, because only "materialist reflectionism" will decide
the question on who is to rule the country and the world.

History, Mao has said, was made by slaves, that is, the
proletariat, and not be geniuses and heroes, by which he
means the bourgeoisie. Key words in Mao's process history
are "perpetual revolution" (a concept recently put to rest
by the present leadership) and "the dictatorship of the
proletariat."

At this point, the reasoning process tightens. Because
the Chinese Communist Party represents the proletariat, it
will rule forever and it will rule alone. But, in fact,
who rules? "The masses," says the government. It is well
known that the founder of the Chinese Communist Party and
its leader until he was purged, Chen Duxiu, held a different view. In his The Origin of the Chinese Communist Party
(Taipei: Democratic Wave, 1959, p. 83), he writes: "There
was no such thing as the 'dictatorship by the proletariat.'
There was dictatorship by the Party. In the end, it was
dictatorship by the leader." Which, come to think of it,
may be part of Marxism's sinification.

It is well to remember at this point, as Richard C.
Bush, Jr., aptly remarks, that "almost anyone who speaks
about Chinese history observes that Chinese tradition,
culture, philosophy... in spite of invasions by barbarians,
Manchus, Japanese, or the West, always manages to reassert
itself." (p. 380) Professor Tsien, who specializes at Paris
in Chinese political history, remarks that the great communist themes dominate the Chinese ideological scene. He
feels that Mao's specific contribution was "that of

synthesizing a revolutionary practice which serves as scientific experimentation to theory."(p. 46) As Steve S.K. Chin has convincingly argued in his The Thought of Mao Tse-tung, Form and Content, Hong Kong: Centre of Asian Studies, 1979, it is ridiculous to maintain that every aspect of Mao's thought stems either from Confucius or from some Chinese philosophical school. Mao's synthesis between Marxism and Chinese thought bears the hallmark of his genius.

In line with the above, I should now like to advert to the famous "theory of contradictions," another of Mao's contributions to Marxist ideology. Briefly, according to this theory, society progresses only through the solution of unceasing contradictions. One must first analyze and divide these contradictions in antagonistic and non-antagonistic ones, all the time remembering that the principal and secondary characteristics of each contradiction are in constant change. In other words, contradictions are of the yin-yang type, i.e., they complement one another. Hence, in Mao's vocabulary, "contradiction" is synonymous of "relation." Marxism tries to dissolve "antagonistic contradictions," the main one of which is the opposition between the masses and their enemies. Through class struggle, enemies will be vanquished, and the basic contradiction will disappear.

There is, in China as elsewhere, an "existential necessity" which leads to reconciliation of contradictions, lest the nation perish. One understands perfectly well what Vice-premier Deng has in mind: on the one hand, he finds it necessary to subordinate the individual, as totally as possible, to the needs and dictates of the Marxist state; and on the other hand, he is aware of the need to foster individualism, personal initiative and inventiveness as an essential component of growth in a neo-capitalist state-economy. If the individual were subordinated by crude repression, this would expose the mythological character of Marxist freedom. Understandably then, a call to duty above class, by which is meant unqualified loyalty to the Party, becomes the theoretical basis of a new morality, the only one acceptable to the state. Marx, in fact, took this principle from Kant; and it has been applied, with equal ruthlessness, in some capitalist as well as in some Marxist societies.

Mao recognized no source of moral principles that depend upon criteria outside historical society, such as would be the Commandments of a Christian God. Hence, he knew very well that religion, and particularly Christianity, remains always in "antagonistic contradiction" with dialectical materialism. Mao's moral outlook, if I understand him correctly, implies the principle of "the greatest possible good for the greatest possible number," a principle which is but another way of stating the maxim that "the end justifies the means." If Mao now be asked: "What justifies the

end?", he might point out that, during the last thirty
years, the question is irrelevant because, in practical
Chinese life, the end and the means constantly converge,
even change places. Mao thought of himself as having the
charisma of discovering biological-social instincts in
the masses. To him, morality is the product of social
environment; hence, there is nothing immutable in it. At
all times, it must serve social interests, and these interests feed on "contradictions."

Morality, more than any other form of ideology, bears
the stamp of class. The bourgeois -- and the Christian --
social ethic which transcends sectional class interest is
unacceptable. In fact, it must be unmasked as an ever-
present element in the mechanics of class deception.

What might appear as Maoist amoralism is, in fact, in
Mao's eyes, a pseudonym for a higher type of morality, the
morality of class war. That is permissible which leads to
the abolition of power of man over man. Since this end
can only be achieved through revolution, the liberating
morality of the Chinese proletariat is, of necessity, en-
dowed with a revolutionary aura. Thereby it irreconcil-
ably banishes all dogma, and all kinds of idealistic fe-
tishes which are the philosophical gendarmes of the ruling
class.

All the above is an echo of speeches heard at the June
1979 People's Congress. Obviously, as long as this theory-
cum-practice speaks to the same historical situation, it
will be maintained. Should the situation change, the theory will change with the situation, not so much in theory,
but in practice. Basically then, a good Maoist is a good
"revisionist." And the possibility of change, even in matters of religion, cannot, in principle and in practice, be
excluded. Which, in itself, should be to Christians a matter of modest hope.

+

+   +

Christians still have another reason for hope. The
Kingdom of God, they believe, is already with us. This
Kingdom has nothing in common with Hegel's Absolute. As a
Christian, I feel, I can perfectly well understand the
background of Mao's interesting statement made a few months
before his death to Belgium's Prime-minister Leo Tindemans:
"For me, God is the Chinese people!" The Kingdom is no static philosophical abstraction looming high at the horizon of
history. It is a dynamic reality already incarnated in the
person of Jesus Christ. And, peace be to Mao, through the
love of Jesus Christ for them, it also reaches the Chinese
people through and through.

Christians, in China and everywhere, hold this faith in earthen vessels; they live this faith in sweat and tears, in suffering and death. We, outsiders to the Chinese situation, look up to them with reverence and deep empathy. We feel, with them, that Maoism is not the final goal of man. At the same time, we agree that it is an attempt toward the abolition of class society, and of all kinds of oppression, to which the Chinese people have been subjected throughout the centuries.

Hence, I submit, no doubt in my ignorance, that, in China, a revolutionary Christian -- and nothing in his faith prevents a Christian from being a "revolutionary" in the example of Christ -- might look upon the class struggle as a necessary means towards the liberation of his people, and of the world. As a "revolutionary," the Christian does not need specifically "Christian" criteria for the conduct of that struggle. Properly understood, and prudently applied, the principles of socialism, as seen by Mao, need not inevitably conflict with Christian principles of morality. Between them, I hope and pray, there is no "antagonistic contradiction." As Christianity and China stand face to face, there is no call for the extermination of the one or of the other. There only is a call for mutual understanding and collaboration.

THE PLACE OF MYSTERY AND TRANSCENDENCE

The third issue that needs to be examined when Christians from China and the United States get together is the place of mystery and transcendence within Chinese art, music, literature and family life. We know there are stirrings in western culture and also East European culture in the area of mystery and transcendence. One of the remarkable changes in the last few years has been within Marxist countries. There is a new interest and concern for things of this kind in their philosophy and in their understanding of where their people are hurting. This is also true in European and North American cultures as the people struggle with the problem of technology, the dehumanization of the urban areas and the deepening alienation between the poor and the rich, the minorities and the majorities, men and women.

Tracey K. Jones, in Occasional Bulletin,
July 1979, p. 91.

PART TWO:

CHURCH AND CHINA LOOK ONE ANOTHER IN THE EYES

I now turn more specifically to recent aspects of the encounter between China and the Church. I am aware of the
fact that both "China" and "Church" are comprehensive terms
deserving an integrated treatment much more acceptable than
these pages can afford to give. So much more remains to be
said, but it cannot all be said at this time. In sum, Church
and China are in midstride of a grave crisis. The pages which
follow explore some elements of that crisis. In full loyalty
to either side involved, they invite the reader to pray with
me for an eventual solution.

As in Part One, there is a need for selection and priorities. My priorities are set within the limits indicated in
the Preface; they bathe in a mood of reconciliation which,
as the days go by, impresses itself ever more strongly on
my mind. This mood feeds on convergent probabilities, on
convergent possibilities, and on convergent, sometimes even
contradictory, bits of information. Hence, there is nothing
apodictical in my approach, and nothing irreformable in my
conclusions.

Chapter 1:

Christians on China: trying to understand
_____

    While I was in Hong Kong at the beginning of 1979, the
air was abuzz with exciting news. By way of example, here
is part of a news release distributed by the Shanghai City
Information Service on January 11:

> Religious figures met in Shanghai on January 9, angrily
> denouncing Lin Biao and the Gang of Four for their
> counter-revolutionary crimes in trampling on the legal
> system, undermining the Party's policy on religions
> and ruthlessly persecuting religious believers. This
> was the first meeting of people in religious circles
> since they suspended activities more than ten years
> ago. Eight hundred patriotic personages of the Roman
> Catholic, Protestant, Buddhist and Islamic faiths, to-
> gether with comrades concerned with the departments of
> religions, attended the meeting.

We were further told that the Gang of Four destroyed
churches and burned a large quantity of valuable records.
The Shanghai meeting insisted that charges against religious leaders be withdrawn, and their reputations restored.
The communique ends with these words: "The Shanghai Religious Affairs Bureau will be reopened and unite the masses
of religious believers behind the program of the Four Modernizations."

    It is not difficult to scrape off the ideological cant
of this declaration and have it say what it means: Religious freedom is back -- although within the limits of the
law, and for the sake of the Four Modernizations. What
these limits could be was spelled out a few months later
by Deng Xiaoping himself in a characteristic phrase: "In
China religion is free. I couldn't care less about people's belief as long as they observe the law and work hard."

Small wonder that the spring air was humming with sounds
of hope. All sorts of "official" hints were thrown out to
fuel that hope. In December 1978, some pastors who had
joined the Three Self Movement received a small gift of
money "in recognition of your services." In fact, I was
told, the money reached them on Christmas. At the Hong
Kong-Canton border, visitors were informed that the Bible
was no longer on the list of forbidden books; in fact,
each person could bring in as many as 100 copies without
raising official eyebrows. Permission to visit China was
readily granted to Christian dignitaries. A sporadic revi-
val of public worship was reported, particularly among
Protestants. In the coastal city of Suatou, on Christmas
1978, hundreds of people tried to crowd into the delapida-
ted Catholic church. The officiating priest was so fright-
ened that he begged the crowd to go away.

The full range of the new China-and-Church relations
came in for serious scrutiny at the First Chinese Theologians' Colloquium which took place in Hong Kong, February
2-10, 1979, and which I was privileged to attend. The
cream of diaspora China theologians, Catholic and Protestant, met at the local Catholic seminary to review the
situation and come up with practical suggestions for future
contact between China and Christianity. I was impressed
by many things: the talents and youthfulness of the fifty
participants; their love for China and for the Church; and
their efforts to transcend our old confessional divisions.
All of a sudden, in my mind, a hundred theological flowers
began to bloom. To give the reader an idea of the buoyant
mood in which we worked, here is part of the report submitted to the plenary by the workshop on "Political Theology":

We note the increased participation of China in global
affairs, and the renewal of relationships on many levels.
We are fearful of repeating the tragic errors which have
beset the history of Christian missions in China. Hence,
we must carefully evaluate this history to feel the
sharpness of the Chinese-Marxist critique of Christianity.
We must learn from our fellow Christians in China about
their faith and witness, their patterns of Church life
and ministry. Unless we accept a transformation of our
own theology, our understanding of mission, and our life
style, we may again impose upon China the travesty of a
Christianity which is sectarian, highly institutionalized,
culturally imperialist and class-confirmed.

At this and all previous theological meetings, there was
much attention given to what we used to call "the missionary role of the Church." But none of us ever advocated
"the return of missionaries." Quite to the contrary, we
strongly deprecated sending into China anyone for the

purpose of proselytism. And we insistently pleaded in
favor of leaving, in this matter, the initiative in Chinese hands.

This stand may cause surprise, particularly when it comes
from a former Catholic missionary to China. It may also
cause disbelief, witness Bishop Ting's paper below. But it
is dead serious, and I can only repeat that our longing to
have the universal Church enriched by full fellowship with
a fully alive Chinese Christianity does not have us call
for a traditional missionary return to China.

One of the reasons, as our China congresses have always
pointed out, is that the world Church is still often en-
meshed in an unjust world system which compromises the
power of the Gospel. Christians rarely, if ever, manifest
the joy, forgiveness and unity in such a shining way that
it will lend credibility to their words. We do not yet
know how to learn from an ancient culture, such as that of
China, now being transformed; nor do we know how to speak
in tones that it cares to hear.

But this does not mean that we see no place for preaching
the Gospel in China. To the contrary, we strongly believe
that the very nature of the Chinese revolution proves the
need for the Gospel to keep it radical, honest, and humane.
As we see it, a Church worthy of the new China is a Church
steeped in the Chinese tradition, soaked in the thought and
life of the new China, and eager to understand the aspira-
tions of the Chinese people in the light of Christ's redeem-
ing message to all mankind.

A Church worthy of the new China calls for the corporate
disassociation from all unjust structures, even where the
Church's privileged position might be threatened. It means
judging carefully in each situation what forces are for
true progress; and it means supporting those forces at the
risk of making mistakes. It means stopping the use of the
central gift of God through Jesus Christ, the forgiveness
of sins, as a cover-up for injustice instead of its use for
individual, social, and corporate renewal. It means developing, in, with, and for China, a theology whose source is
not dependence upon imported systems of thought but upon
the serious and free reflection of the whole Christian community on the wrenching experiences of the last thirty
years, so that we all may witness with authentic selfhood
to what Christ means for China.

As a Catholic, I believe that this task involves the whole
Church, and not only, as some would claim, the Christians
of China with the exclusion of fellow Christians around the
world, particularly the Pope. The Catholic Church, first and
foremost, is communion -- with Peter.

Obviously, the nature of Christian togetherness with China remains to be worked out. Such a togetherness will give full consideration to the government's legitimate insistence on national independence and dignity; it will be predicated on the unity and reconciliation of all Chinese Christians, and not only of any faction; finally, it will preserve, for China and for the Church at large, the essentials of our faith.

1. Contemporary China: a theological challenge

The very existence of Maoist China, one-quarter of mankind that is, doggedly building a new world, uninfluenced by, and even inimical to, the Christian churches is a fact of tremendous theological importance. The mystery of this fact is compounded by the image which China projects upon the world, an ambiguous image, no doubt, but yet an image so eloquently attractive to millions of people that they look up to it as to an alternative type of society in which more men and women shall have access to elementary human freedom and wellbeing than is now the case.

Contemporary China, as a theological fact, has been the subject of all our China meetings, from Bastad, Sweden, January 1974, to Male, Belgium, September 1979. Since the conference in Leuven, September 1974, Catholics now meet under the umbrella of a group called "Catholics in Europe Concerned with China" (CECC). In October 1976, the Congregation for the Evangelization of Peoples hosted a meeting on China and set up a China Study Center. There are parallel efforts on the Protestant side, often mediated by the Lutheran World Federation's office in Geneva. We rejoice in an excellent ecumenical collaboration which, I feel, sets an example for other sectors in the Church.

I should now like to consider some elements of the theological challenge which China presents to the Christian faith, and then come to what, in my opinion, could be our ecumenical response.

Let me make three introductory remarks. First, the distinction between theological considerations and an ecumenical response is only valid for the sake of argument and method. In fact, "to do theology" means "to do theology ecumenically." Anything less falls short of "doing" and of "theology." Second, the challenge to which I refer, although it comes directly from China, is not confined to China because, what goes under the name of Maoist thought has an appeal throughout the world. Third, this challenge would not disappear even if China should negate her recent past. There is a new China, be it in full and unpredictable evolution. There shall be a new China for the Church, whether its doors be closed or widely opened. Free and immediate access to China would not change this fact; it would only add urgency to our Christian response.

China needs the Church, because it needs Christ whose sacrament is the Church. The Church needs to be in China because of her mission to all the children of God. To the Church, no human being is a stranger or an enemy. China needs the Church, not to save it from Communism, but to save Communism from its man-made limitations. China and the Church should become partners in building human happiness and dignity throughout the world. At present their ways have parted. But this estrangement need not last, and Christian hope tells us that it shall not last. It may end soon; or it may come about after a long and laborious gestation of mutual respect and empathy.

If and when this situation should change, Christians pray and hope that China's new attitude towards Christianity will be due, not to political or economic factors tantamount to a new type of religious gunboat diplomacy, but to the sheer attractiveness, humanism and general usefulness of the Christian way of life as seen by Chinese eyes. It is definitely within the limits of historical possibilities -- think of Christianity's history in Japan -- that, after their long travail, Chinese Christians may have grown to a new dimension of faith from which the Church universal has much to learn.

Our China meetings, Protestant, Catholic or ecumenical, have mostly based their conclusions on an analysis of what is to us a painful, and sometimes inglorious past. These conclusions must be retained. But, I submit, they must also be inserted in the flow of history and take stock of the new, perhaps imminent, possibilities to which I have referred. With that prospect in mind, and at considerable risk, let me present some items on a practical shopping list of theological goods which the new China might well present to Christianity.

a. A fair sense of sociological realism

We know very little about the real, the human, China. Our sources of information remain erratic, uncontrollable, probably unreliable. Personal contact is improving, but information, at the beginning of 1980, is still highly conditioned, sporadic and selective. Scientific inquiry into the quality of happiness or the quantity of grief

which are the measure of the humaneness of any society --
and hence, of the relative presence or absence of fruits
of the Holy Spirit in that society -- this is still at
present a theologian's impossible dream. However difficult the hermeneutics of the China situation, the Church
wants to know the facts, all the facts. But factual knowledge remains sterile, in Christian as well as in Maoist
thinking, unless it be brought to life within the framework of an interpretation both charitable and correct.
Such a framework calls for an initial meeting of minds,
Maoist and Christian, on the existential interrelationship
between thought and action.

As is well known, in this matter Maoists distinguish
three stages: theory, ideology, and praxis.

1. Theory: By this Maoists mean the ideal shape of
   things into which reality must be transformed. In
   the final analysis, the utopia which they pursue,
   whatever could be said about its cost and means,
   resembles the Christian search for transcendentals:
   truth, goodness and beauty, expressed in patterns
   of decent living, dignity, loyalty and self-reliance.

2. Ideology: This refers to the body of principles
   which help transform reality into the longed-for
   ideal. Such a process requires an analysis of
   objectives, both theoretical and practical, aiming
   at the creation of a new and better reality which
   straddles the whole field of human activities, private and communal. Maoists dream of a new society,
   based on service and equality; they call for a new
   ethics, a new pedagogy, a new social psychology, in
   which priority goes to the masses rather than to
   the individual; to that effect, they enforce new
   methods of information and new patterns of cultur-
   alization.

3. Praxis: Christians are eager to examine the practical
   achievements of the PRC over the last thirty years.
   They want to do this in objective historical perspective through careful listening, and, partly at least,
   on Maoist terms. The main topics for such an analysis
   might be some such as the following:

   -- Within the social field: liberation from western
      imperialism and colonialism; equality for men and
      women; the new concept of marriage; the communes
      and a new style of life attentive to everyone's
      minimum needs; health and educational developments.

-- Within the political field: the new bureaucratic and the legal structure; the Party and the military; nationalism and internationalism; the shape of foreign policy.

-- Within the economic field: freedom from extreme want and domination; advances in agriculture, industry and mining, technology and finances.

-- Within the cultural field: the interacting of rural and urban populations, of peasants and intellectuals; the power of the masses and of the Party; the alternating rhythm of occupational activities; the ascetic life within a non-consumerist society; etc.

The theological evaluation of theory, ideology, and praxis, even if ample information were freely available, would be a gigantic task. It is also a task for which our present theologians are ill-prepared. This task is much too complex and important to be done by westerners; it calls for an effort of worldwide collaboration to which the remnants of the Church in China must bring their irreplaceable contribution.

b. Sympathy for what unites; a clear eye for what divides

The theologian in search for values in Maoist China needs an excellent grasp on recent advances in Christian philosophy and theology, particularly as they relate to man and society, which is the this-worldly core of Maoist thought. This comparative and interdisciplinary study will want to plumb, at the hand of authentic Gospel standards, the spiritual meaning of Maoist reality, in theory, ideology and practice. Some pathways of this research might look as follows:

1. At the theoretical level:

-- An integrated view of orthodoxy and orthopraxis, both in Maoism and in Christianity. On the Christian side, this could lead to a reinterpretation of what is basic in the Christian faith in an effort to express it in dynamic and dialectical categories accessible to Maoist thought. The Chinese people, I feel, remain open to an incarnational theology in spite of their avowed atheism and anti-religionism.

-- A comparative theology of society and of sociopolitical structures; of patterns of liberation vs. patterns of oppression, applied to the individual, the local and the national community.

-- A critical inventory and assimilation of recent
western, Latin American and African theologies
sometimes congenial to the Maoist perception of
reality. One thinks here of elements in Moltmann's
Theology of Hope which is inspired by the Marxist
philosopher Ernst Bloch; of the Political Theology
of J.B. Metz; of Joseph Comblin's Theology of Revolution; of Gustavo Gutierrez's Theology of Liberation... One thinks of parallel efforts related
to Marxism such as the books of Garaudy, Ellul and
many others. Finally, one thinks of Freire's conscientization pedagogy, and of Illich's deschool-
ing.

2. At the ideological level:

The above theologies and worldviews are concerned
with the relation between theory and ideology.
In the Maoist perception of religion, they do imply
a goodly measure of Christian self-criticism made by
loyal Christians of the expression, imperfect and
always time- and culture-bound, of their faith. These
theologies deprecate all compromise of the Church
with liberalistic ideologies, with power structures,
wealth and oppression, in sum, with all those evil
concomitants often identified with religion in the
western world. Thereby they try to witness to a
Gospel which does not succumb to one static ideology of whichever name; they refuse to accept a mono-
cultural, i.e., western, expression of the Christian
truth and ethos. Rather, they insist upon the need
for contextualization of a Christianity which, like
Christ himself, bears the hallmark of a transcendence open to every culture and ideology. These
theologies try to interpret the social doctrine of
the Church according to the socio-economic realities
of the culture within which they originate. They
recognize the truth of what Pope Paul VI said in
reference to Maoist China on December 7, 1965:

The religion of God who became man has encountered
the religion -- for it is a religion -- of man who
became God. What came out of this encounter?
Shock, anathema? No. We too have the cult of man.
Our humanism becomes Christianity, and our Christianity is theocentrical to the point that we
dare say: "To know God, one must know man."

Theology must get to know Maoist man with that gnosis
which is inspired by the Christian hope in the Holy

Spirit, renovans faciem terrae; renovating China and the
Church. No one doubts that the Spirit breathed where he
wills, also in China whence, almost apocalyptically, he is
now speaking the the churches.

3. At the practical level:

A practical approach to this program of theological
research is of supreme importance to the Maoist mind,
and, may I add, also to the Christian view of life.
Yet here is the rub. Too often, Christians have
shielded themselves behind an abstract or inteelectu-
alistic facade of their faith. Often they have failed to see that orthodoxy needs authentication by
orthopraxis; and that love becomes believable only
through acts of love. Some of the arduous but practical goals at which a China-directed Christian theology might aim are the following:

-- The conscientization of the churches leading to an
   adjustment of their mentality and attitudes towards
   China.

-- An increased and systematic contact of the churches
   with China, whenever and wherever possible, on the
   mainland and in the diaspora of 47-million Chinese,
   many of whom are Christians with increased access to
   their families on the continent.

-- A search for convergences between Chinese and Christian ideals related to the human person. In a Teil-
   hardian perspective such a search, seemingly start-
   ing at possible poles, may meet within the Incarnation, the Supreme Reality of God-made-man.

-- A continuing interest in China, commensurate to her
   numbers and importance, nurtured within the churches
   by a spirit of prayer, penance and reconciliation.

-- Thoughtful attention to the situation and the role
   of Christian communities in Taiwan.

-- The striving for a new style of Christian life, attractive to the Chinese people through its asceti-
   cism, non-exploitative emulation, disdain for wealth
   and comfort, rank and honor; which all adds up to
   the active sharing of one's avoir, pouvoir, and
   savoir in the service of one's neighbor.

In summary, China challenges Christianity to an authentic
renewal. Maoism is providentially, if unwillingly, cast in
a prophetic role. This call for renewal rings loud in all
the churches, old or new, foreign or Chinese; and they must
heed it together.

2. China: an exciting ecumenical opportunity

Our China meetings have powerfully impressed their participants with the fact that, faced with the momentous reality of China, our sectarian divisions make no sense, and
that they must stop before, in the phrase often heard at
Leuven, "the Church could be worthy of the New China."

My immediate concern here is to say something about ecumenical attitudes and actions in the Church at large, and
not about what such actions could be among Christians in
the PRC, about which I lack sufficient information.

There are principles and stages underlying the Christian
search for unity in regard to China, all of them falling
within the general orbit of today's ecumenical movement in
its local, national and international manifestations. In
general, the following plan for action seems to me to be
both urgent and feasable:

1. An initial coordination could result from the formation of Christian joint committees in Asia,
   Europe and North America. Some such groups already
   exist; they greatly facilitate an exchange of information between experts working for the churches;
   and they have helped shape church policy.

2. The challenging of all church efforts related to
   China through one or more ecumenical clearinghouses
   in each continent, assuring a flow of mutual information, establishing research and contact priorities, and preventing overlapping and duplication.

3. An integrated effort by the churches to arrive at
   a large area of consensus related to eventual possibilities for further service to China.

4. An intensive study of the linguistic and cultural
   aspects which fruitful contact with China presup-
   poses, such as the preparation of specialists, pre-
   ferably of Chinese ancestry, willing to work with
   the churches; the preparation of Chinese literature
   specifically written for the Chinese masses.

5. The elaboration and the mutual acceptance of
   ecumenical guidelines underlying renewed Christian contact with China, based on the conviction
   that we do not aim at a pragmatic type of unity
   to facilitate the reentry of Christian missionaries into China but rather at a convincing expression of a theological fact: our unity in
   Christ, our membership in the same Body, our
   common vocation to serve the Chinese nation.

This is an open-ended list to which our China conferences have added their own suggestions. As one who has spent
many years in ecumenical activities, I'm aware how difficult it is in ecumenical matters to shift from theory to
action. I am also aware that new opportunities for closer
relationship with Christians in China are bound to become
the acid test of our ecumenical earnest. Finally, I wonder
to what extent former divisions of Christians in the PRC
as well as more recent causes of disunity will influence
the goal which with all of us should rate priority: "That
we may be one."

"THEOLOGICAL REFLECTION FOCUSES ON SUCH QUESTIONS AS .."

a. Will Three-Self Movement pastors or "Christian"
   workers who betrayed the brethren be saved?
   Should these "Judases" be forgiven, or rejected?

b. Should believers have any fellowship with Seventh
   Day Adventists and True Jesus Church people, whom
   they regard as sects?

c. How can baptism and the Lord's supper be handled
   when there are no ordained pastors around to per-
   form these?

d. What is the place of suffering in the believer's
   life? How should Christians interpret the meaning
   of such prolonged suffering in China?

e. What should be the relationship between believers
   who have survived 20 years' imprisonment for their
   faith and those who avoided this be keeping their
   faith quiet? What should their attitudes and approaches be toward those who fell from their faith
   while under pressure?

Jonathan Chao, Partnerscan, June 1979, p. 14

Chapter 2:

Religion in the China of Hua and Deng

Before describing the actual state of religions in the
PRC, it is necessary to clear to air of certain misunderstanding often found in the foreign press. Hence, these
four questions: 1. What is the official view of religion?
2. What is the relationship between religion and ideology?
3. What is the difference between religion and superstition? and 4. Is Maoism a religion? After giving a short answer to each of these questions, I shall then proceed to a
brief look at the state of China's religions at the end of
this year.

1. What is the communist view of religion?

Between the fall of the Manchu dynasty in 1911 and the
communist conquest of China in 1949, the Chinese people,
and particularly the intellectuals, showed an increased
indifference towards the traditional religions to the point
that many observers felt religion would fade away. At
first, the Communists thought so too. Yet they took no
chances and decided actively to accelerate the demise of
religion. They issued crippling regulations. Under Mao's
personal guidance a theoretical approach to religion was
worked out. This approach culminated in extremely repressive measures under the Gang of Four, particularly during
the Cultural Revolution. The official view was and remains that religion is "a function common to feudal societies" and that it is doomed to die in a socialist state.

Tour guides put it like this: "Religion in China is dead.
There are temples and churches, but no one is interested."
In other words, to hear them, the social roots of religion
have disappeared. Be it remarked that religion in China
has traditionally been weak and that it offered little or
no resistance.

The official theory on religion insists that it is a
weapon used by landlords and missionaries to exploit the

masses, call for submission to their miserable fate, and
wean them from the class struggle which is needed so they
may achieve a better life. (BR, 12/2:15) Apart from these
"social roots" of religion, there are also "cognitive
roots." Through science and ideological awareness, man's
thirst for religion will disappear.

As religion in China is bound to die a natural death,
its recent repression often had an air of indecision and
no intensive atheistic propaganda was attempted because
"religion will destroy itself." The Party slogan which
describes this policy is "to seek common ground while re-
taining differences." The last several months, the government even solicits "the wholehearted collaboration" of
religion. What a few years ago appeared to be an "antagonistic contradiction" is no longer so. Differences in
"ideological awareness" between believers and non-believers
are no deterrent to their mutual relations. The factual
oppression of religion in the recent past, it is now said,
is "nonantagonistic" to collaboration in the present.

The latest semi-official statement on "Policy on religion" is found in BR, 12/21:14-22. Its author is Xiao Wen,
and what he writes is, word for word, almost identical
with the PD, 3/15 editorial analyzed below, so much so
that, I feel, Xiao Wen is Xiao Xienfa, the powerful official who heads the Religious Affairs Bureau in Beijing.
What Xiao writes is by now the classic expression of the
nature and function of religion in the PRC. As will be
seen below, this expression is on the lips of Christians
as well. Hence it is essential that it be read carefully
as an outstanding example of that ritual or stereotyped
kind of language in which official China tries to express
itself. Hence, the long quotation which follows needs no
apology.

In 1945, Comrade Mao Zedong said: "All religions are
permitted in China's Liberated Areas, in accordance
with the principle of freedom of religious belief.
All believers in Protestantism, Catholicism, Islamism,
Buddhism and other faiths enjoy the protection of the
people's government so long as they are abiding by
its laws. Everyone is free to believe or not to believe...

In the semi-feudal and semi-colonial old China, churches were under the control of imperialism and monasteries and temples were connected with the feudal system of exploitation. After nationwide liberation,
Party and state leaders received on many occasions
religious representatives, encouraging them to oppose
imperialism, love the country, and make greater

contributions to the socialist motherland. Since
then, in accordance with the wishes of the believers, they set up their religious bodies or patriotic organizations with the support of the people's
government. These organizations engaged in massive
patriotic movements to oppose imperialism, which
ended the control of churches by Chinese or foreign
exploiting classes, and did away with feudal privileges enjoyed by religious rulers and their oppression and exploitation. Religious bodies functioned
on their own and democratically ran their own churches. Proper religious activities were carried on
normally.

However, religious freedom was practically non-
existent when Lin Biao and the Gang of Four held
sway. In order to restore the Party's religious
policy, Article 147 of the Criminal Law, which was
promulgated last July and is to come into force as
from January 1, 1980, stipulates:

A state functionary who unlawfully deprives a
citizen of his legitimate freedom of religious
belief or violates the customs and folkways of
a minority nationality, to a serious degree,
shall be sentenced to imprisonment for not more
than two years, or to detention.

Article 165 stipulates:

A sorcerer or witch who uses superstition to
spread rumors or to fraudulently acquire money
or articles shall be sentenced to imprisonment
for not more than two years, or to detention,
or to public surveillance or, in serious cases,
to imprisonment for two to seven years.

These regulations guarantee by law the citizen's
right to freedom of religion.

Mr Xiao then returns to the penal aspects of the new law:

Anyone who distorts religious policy, or carries on
illegal activities in the name of religion, result-
ing in disrupting social order, or production or
normal day-to-day life, must be given education and
their activities stopped. Those who violate the
law to a serious degree must be punished according
to the law.

Mr Xiao asks further: "Why has the Chinese Government
laid down the above-mentioned policies on religious
affairs?" He answers his own question with an authentic
definition of Marxist atheism:

Marxists are atheists. They hold that religion is
idealism, which runs diametrically counter to materialism and science. But on the other hand, religion,
being a product of history, has its own objective law
governing its origin, development and passing away.
It is a social ideology. The basic reason of its origin and existence is rooted in natural oppression and
social oppression, as well as in people failing to
find explanations to these two oppressions. They
therefore seek help from mystic power. Religion makes
the working people put up with adverse circumstances
and fatalistic in their struggle against nature and in
     the class struggle. That is why Marxists hold that
religion is opium which lulls the will of the people.

In the period of socialism, the social and ideological origin of religion still exists, religion will
still be around for a considerable time. Banning
religious activities will only lead to more primitive
superstitious activities, overtly or covertly.

For Mr Xiao "religious belief is an ideological problem
and a private matter of an individual." Yet, he insists:

There are differences between those who believe in or
not believe in religion, between those who believe in
this religion or that religion, but it does not prevent them from uniting together to work for the Four
Modernizations. The government will on no account
take administrative measures to force people not to
believe in religion. Only through propaganda and
education and through social practice will people
come to the correct conclusion as to whether accept
religion or not, believe in superstition or science,
idealism or materialism, which are diametrically opposed, and free themselves of mental fetters.

No article, or speech, is complete nowadays without a
blast at the evil Gang of Four, and one gains the impression that, to blame the Gang of Four for all and every
problem in the PRC, confers upon the speaker instantly
the stamp of Maoist orthodoxy. Mr Xiao is no exception to
that rule:

When the Gang of Four ran amuck, its members sabotaged
the state policy on religion, declaring that religion
"no longer exists." Under the influence of their ultra-
Left line, normal religious beliefs and activities
were obstructed. Monasteries, temples and churches
were closed down or demolished. Religious personages
were persecuted and customs and habits of certain
minority nationalities were even wantonly interfered
with.

The three years after the downfall of the Gang of Four
saw the policy of freedom of religious belief being
reimplemented. Clerics have returned to the monasteries, temples and churches to handle religious affairs
and carry on religious activities. Famous monasteries,
temples and churches have been gradually repaired and
reopened. Many victimized religious personages have
been rehabilitated and some have been reinstated in
their former posts. (BR, 12/21)

Mr Xiao knows what he is talking about. He himself is
one of these officials; and so is also Mr Tang Lidao, the
General Secretary of the Catholic Patriotic Association.

2. What is the relationship between religion and ideology?

Mao thought that religion was the product of historical
circumstances, and, with the change of those circumstances,
religion would disappear. In fact, Mao had considerable
patience with the slow pace of religious change. In his
famous Report on an Investigation of the Peasant Movement
in Hunan, March, 1927, Mao asserted that:

The statues of idols have been set up by the peasants
and, at a certain date, the peasants shall know how to
get rid of them; they need not be taken away prematurely.

And again, in February 1957, the Great Helmsman showed a
fair degree of tolerance when he remarked in his "On the Correct Handling of Contradictions among the People": "We cannot abolish religion by administrative decrees; we cannot
oblige people not to believe." On this he was dead right.

Communist theoreticians neatly distinguish between ideology,
which they also call philosophy in their publications desti-
ned for the West, and religion, which they also call theology.
Philosophy explains the basic truths on man and his world.
It is rational and logical; while religion is a figment of the
mind which rests on faith, and not on facts. In the case of
Christianity, for example, religion has no need to justify
itself. Christians say that God is their justification.

Although opposed by their very nature, religion and philosophy sometimes do meet. Religion may then appeal to philosophy to bolster its prestige with the masses; philosophy
may then exploit religion, thereby better to exploit the
people.

As an example of the former case, Party scholars refer to
thomism and neo-thomism, while the positivism of Auguste Comte

is an example of the latter. In fact, similar cases abound
in Chinese history.

First, there is Confucianism, the philosophical school of
the literati, founded by Confucius (551-479 B.C.), and almost
exterminated by China's unifier, Emperor Qin-shihuangdi. The
philosopher Dong Chungshu (179-104 B.C.) came to its rescue
by tying Confucius' doctrines to metaphysical considerations
sych as "the five elements," and the fatalistic doctrine of
"the will of Heaven." Confucianism soon became the "religion
of the ruling class," without, however, "becoming a real religion." (Mao, Selected Works, I, p. 313)

Similar is the case of Taoism, a philosophy developed by
Lao Zi in the Daodejing. In the second century A.D., Taoism
assimilates all sort of ill-digested elements of Buddhism
and popular superstitions, and thereby becomes a religion.

The case of Buddhism, Islam, and Christianity is different.
These foreign imports were never seen as philosophies. Buddhism is the "religion of Buddha" (Fo-jiao), Islam is that
of the Hui (Hui-jiao), and Christianity is that of Christ
(Jidu-jiao).

The fusion of religion and philosophy points to the degeneration of philosophy. Mao Zedong's thought is pure philosophy, totally untainted by religion. This thought rests
on the solid pillar of reason and, hence, it is radically
opposed to systems of faith, and to all sorts of superstition. It is not an absolute in itself, however, and needs
the verification of facts. Unfortunately, not even Mao
Thought is totally immune against degeneration trough religion. As we have seen, the Gang of Four tried to impose
upon Mao's thought religious overtones. At their hands it
quickly became a brand of mysticism and the hotbed of religious fanaticism.

3. What is the difference between religion and superstition?

Xiao Wen, in the article from which I quoted, answers with
this definition:

"Belief in the supernatural and in magic is superstition.
Religion is superstitious, but superstition is not equivalent to religion." He then goes on to say that:

By religion we mainly refer to Protestantism, Islamism,
Buddhism and other faiths that have a long history and
have a wide influence among the people in many countries.
Each has its scriptures or holy books, doctrines, rituals
and organizations.

By feudal superstition, we mean sorcery, witchcraft, fortune-telling, palmistry, phrenology, magic and so on. All these are of course absurd and are not believed by those who have some cultural and scientific knowledge. Such feudal and superstitious practices are strictly banned by the government. Those who are hoodwinked to take part in such practices are given education.

Nevertheless, the situation is complicated in real life. Some people are accustomed to such practices as worshipping ancestors, believing in the existence of a soul, spirits and ghosts. So long as their activities do not affect the political and productive activities of the collective, the government will not prevent them by administrative means, but will patiently dissuade them from engaging in such practices. (BR, 12/21:15)

The Beijing Review does not tell us where it got Xiao Wen's article "about China's policy on religion." Actually, it is taken over from an interview of Xiao Xianfa (see p. 64), sent into the world by Xinhua on September 20, and itself going back to an article the Director of the Religious Affairs Bureau first published in the PD of March 15.

The Party has been quite consistent in drawing a sharp dividing line between "superstition," seen as the cult of demons (kuei) and spirits (shen), and "integrated religious systems," such as Buddhism, Islam, and Christianity. It is understood that the "policy of religious freedom" which, since Deng, tries to bring believers and unbelievers together for the sake of the Four Modernizations, does not extend to "superstitions." A statement of considerable importance because it came out after three months of government consultation on the matter, is precisely the editorial column of PD, March 15, to which I have just now referred. (IL, 10:5-7)

Here are some further particulars culled from that statement, and supplemented by more information taken from the PD, 5/27:

Religion is defined as "man's vain and erroneous response to his feelings of impotence and fear in the face of natural and social forces." Marxists have at all times opposed religion which is a tool for the exploitation of the people by their oppressors. The monotheistic religions get a somewhat different appraisal: they originated in slave society and developed in a feudal climate which has now been eliminated. In fact, "all worship or veneration of supernatural forces can be called superstition. All

religions are also superstitions (<u>mixin</u>), but not all
superstitions are religions.

The Chinese government recognizes five religions: 1.
Protestant Christianity; 2. Catholic Christianity;
3. Buddhism; 4. Taoism; 5. Islam. Christianity,
Buddhism and Islam are "the world's three major religions." These religions share the following features:
scriptures, doctrines, rituals, and organization. The
influence of these religions is recognized, particularly on ethnic groups.

Superstition must be suppressed, such as sorcery, palmistry, fortune-telling, phrenology, divination, exor-
cism, praying for children, and so on. These superstitions were almost brought under control before the
Gang of Four came to power. Due to the Gang's des-
tructive policies, they keep disrupting productivity,
causing harm to the people's economy and health.

Mr Xiao concludes his reflections by giving the names of
religious leaders, and among them Wu Yaozong, "the late
president of the National Committee of the Protestant
Churches of China." These leaders "take part in duscussing
state affairs and their opinions are being equally respected."

4. Is Maoism a religion?

My first three questions lead up to the present one to
which I'm forced to carefully weigh my answer. Somewhat
glibly, Alain Peyrefitte writes in his <u>Quand la Chine s'év-
eillera</u> that "le marxisme chinois est une religion du
<u>peuple</u>." I feel that he speaks here as an observer from
the Christian West, and not as an inhabitant of the Middle
Kingdom.

No Chinese in his right mind, after reading Xiao Xianfa
and other specialists, would ever dream of calling Maoism
a "religion." It would be more correct to call it "the supreme controller of all religion." Proof a final paragraph
from the <u>PD</u>, 3/15, already mentioned above:

Religious people must obey the policies and the orders
of the government. They should not impede the freedom
of other believers and of non-believers, nor have a
hand in politics or education, nor do anything whatsoever to return to the system of man's exploitation by
man, a system abolished since the Revolution. It is
forbidden to our enemies to take advantage of religi-

ous practices as a cover-up of counter-revolutionary
or illegal activities. For that reason it is incum-
bent on the government to strengthen its control or
religious organizations.

Dostoevski intuitively knew that the socialism of his
day had assumed religious dimensions: "For socialism is
not merely the labor question; it is before all things
the atheistic question, the question of the form taken
by atheism today, the question of the tower of Babel
built without God, not to mount to heaven from earth,
but to set up heaven on earth." (The Brothers Karamazof,
tr. Constance Carnett, New York: Modern Library, n.d.,
p. 28)

Or perhaps, once more, Mao's theory on contradiction
does apply. A policy which is radically against "religion" or "superstition" as defined by the Chinese government in the name of man's quest for happiness easily
assumes some characteristics of true religion. As such,
it may well satisfy in part man's basic need for justice,
dignity, truth,and goodness. Christians are confident
that the Chinese people will know, and judge the tree by
its fruit.

ASIA-BASED 'CHINESE AND CHURCH' PERIODICALS

from Asia Lutheran News, *special issue n. 2, July 1979*

1. *Asian Report*, Asian Outreach Ltd., GPO Box 3448, HONG KONG. Published monthly in English.

2. *China and the Church Today*, Chinese Church Research Center, 5 Devon Rd. Kowloon, HONG KONG. Published bimonthly in English and *China and the Church* in Chinese.

3. *China News Analysis*, GPO Box 3225, HONG KONG. Published biweekly in English.

4. *China Prayer Letter*, (Address same as No. 2). Published monthly in English/Chinese.

5. *China Talk*, China Liaison Office, World Division, Board of Global Ministries, The United Methodist Church, 2 Man Wan Rd., C-17, Kowloon, HONG KONG. Published in English.

6. *Chinese Around the World*, Chinese Coordination Center of World Evangelism (CCCOWE), 12-14 Hart Ave., 17/F, Kowloon, HONG KONG. Published monthly in English.

7. *Chinese Churches Today*, CCCOWE. (Address same as No. 6). Published monthly in English/Chinese.

8. *Chingfeng*, Tao Fong Shan Christian Study Centre, Shatin, N. T., HONG KONG. Published quarterly in English/Chinese.

9. *Church in China Interview Project Documentary Series*, (Address same as No. 2) Published occasionally and sent only to friends and supporters of the Center. English.

10. *Pray for China*, China Research Center, Christian Communications Ltd. PO Box 95364, Tsimshatsui, HONG KONG. Published bimonthly in English/Chinese.

5. Religions in China: in and after the storm

Here follow a few details on the present state of "religions" in China.

a. Although Confucianism, as we have seen, is not on the
   official list of Chinese religions (and I am not prepared to argue that it is a "religion"), the sinification
of Chinese communism could not be accomplished without
some reference to Confucianism. Although Mao tells us that
he hated Confucius from his youth, it is evident that he
had an excellent grasp of the Confucian classics, references to which abound in his Works. In abetting the campaign
against the Sage, Mao may very well subconciously have
wished to take his place, even though he might have read of
Toynbee's opinion that the Master is "unconquerable."

Be that as it may, Mao knew about the paradoxes raised
by the "unemployed scholars" of Confucius' times; he admired these early revolutionaries and put their inspiration to good use. Two classic examples of such impertinent
makers of paradoxes are the following:

   1. Shen Dao (350-05 B.C.) is a legalist philosopher
      with Taoist overtones who defined knowledge as
      "not to know."

   2. Kongsun Long (b. 380 B.C.?) discoursed on "a white
      horse that is not a horse." (Fung Yu-lan, History
      of Chinese Philosophy, Peiping: Henry Vetch, 1937,
      vol. I, p. 156 and 203-5)

To the present rulers of the PRC, the return of Confucianism poses no real threat. Unlike Taoism, it has rarely
been in the lead of any revolutionary thought. To the contrary, it has always come dressed in the respectable mantle
of conservatism; and, strange though it may sound, at present
a goodly dose of conservatism and cultural continuity could
serve the men in power. It might not matter then, within
the purview of non-antagonistic contradictions, whether the
Chinese people become communists without communism, or
simply Confucianist communists. (Bush: 348-81; Ching: 206)

Visitors report sizeable crowds of worshippers at Qufu,
15 kilometers south of Yangzhou in Shandong province, the
birthplace of Confucius. His descendants are still the
keepers of his temple which suffered some damage during
the Cultural Revolution. Here and there country fairs again
are organized in honor of the Sage. His name is no longer
taboo on the stage. More important, Confucian classics
are again taught in universities, and even studied by the
people.

b. The present rulers feel less kindly toward Taoism.
Statistics put the number of Taoists in 1950 at 30-
million; but this figure is unreliable at best, and no
one knows how many authentic Taoists are alive today.
Hence, I apologize for quoting a somewhat moldy report
which I am unable to verify:

> Contemporary Taoists have been given the spades to dig
> their grave in history. A Taoist Association exists.
> and so the Taoist temples, no longer active and there-
> fore no longer nests of "deceivers," have ceased to be
> "feudal" in the sense of that moralistic epithet; they
> are feudal just in the nomenclature of "scientific his-
> tory." A temple is not a disgrace, but an antique.
> Communists, instead of exhorting the masses to crush
> the infamy, urge them to preserve the relics. That is
> crushing enough. (Klatt: 25)

But that does not mean that the present leaders of China,
much in imitation of Mao whose thought, says Garaudy: 242,
"owes more to the Tao of Lao Zi than to the logics of
Hegel," are oblivious of Taoist inspiration. Indeed, the
influence of Taoism is on the surface of Mao Thought. He
borrowed his famous parable "The Foolish Old Man who Removed the Mountains" from the Taoist book Lie Zi, written
in the 4th century B.C. In 1949, he described the Communist victory as "only the first step in a long march of
ten thousand li" (3 li is 1 mile) knowing very well that
he was paraphrasing the Daodejing, chapter 26, which says
that "The journey of a thousand li starts from where one
stands." His theory on contradiction has a Taoist flavor,
as much as his saying that "one divides in two" which
somehow undergirds Mao's mystique of perpetual revolution
and his efforts at reconciling antithetical positions.
Yet, as in the past, Taoism at present, much like folk
religion which is unadulterated superstition in official
eyes, remain elusive. (Bush: 382-425)

c. Buddhism is the major imported religion of China, thoroughly assimilated in the country's life. Throughout
its long history, Buddhism went through repeated persecu-
tions, the most violent and most disastrous of which may
well have been the most recent, that of the decade 1966-76,
when thousands of temples were destroyed or disestablished
and monks and nuns sent into labor camps around the country. To quote Klatt again, p. 26:

> Religious personalities remain, and they go through
> ritualistic charades at a few selected sites. They
> staff the Chinese Buddhist Association which is as
> tame as its Christian and Taoist counterparts. Like
> them, and like the "democratic parties" in the poli-

tical field, the Association exists to praise the Communists from the outside (the highest accolade), to bear witness to the fact that the revolution is not over, and to give the world a spectacle of communist patience and forbearance.

And Klatt concludes with these words: "All that remains is the historically significant, esthetically valuable, religiously drained antiquities." Many of these antiquities are now well protected against "the imperialist plunderers" of the past; many famous temples, saved during the Cultural Revolution from destruction through the thoughtful intervention of Zhou Enlai, are now under repairs or open to the tourist trade.

Buddhism has its Chinese Buddhist Association, set up by the government, like that of other religions, Islam and Christianity. On the occasion of visits by foreign groups, representatives of these Associations will receive them, much as Bishop Moser was received by the Catholic Patriotic Association in November. (See below) Speeches at such occasions indicate the government line of the moment. As such, they are of interest to our understanding of the atmosphere in which the Associations do their work, and of an eventual shift in policy.

By way of example, let me quote from a report of such a speech by the Buddhist monk Zheng Guo, a member of the Chinese Buddhist Association, at the occasion of the visit by Japanese Buddhist leaders to Beijing, April 23, 1974:

Enemies of our people say that the government aims at the extinction of all religion, but we think that this is not the case. Land reform and democratic revolution do not harm Buddhism. They do not estrange Buddhism from its devotees. Indeed, the very opposite is true. Revolution shakes the dust off Buddhism and purifies it. Hence many Buddhists in China profoundly love the government and rejoice at the present religious policy. (My translation from the Japanese report of Mr Nezu Masuo)

The expression of these sentiments has varied little since the fall of the Gang of Four. Thus Mr Zhao Puchu, speaking for a Chinese Buddhist delegation to Japan in April 1978, said that "since the fall of the Gang of Four, the Chinese Buddhists have greatly increased their activities, assisting the government in the task of repairing temples and setting in order ancient Buddhist texts." (Ta Kung Pao, May 11, 1978) Some of these texts, we are told, will soon come out, much like a new Chinese version of the Bible, in a modern idiom accessible to the people.

One year later, we encounter Mr Zhao Puchu again, but in a very different setting. Zhao is now the head of the Chinese religious delegation to the Third Assembly of the World Conference on Religion and Peace (WCRP) which was held at Princeton, N.J., USA, August 29-September 7, 1979, the delegation to which also Bishop K. H. Ting belonged. (See below)

The Chinese delegation participated in a press conference in New York, August 28, at which Mr Zhao had this message:

> As our friends may have known, China is a multi-religious country. The major religions are Buddhism, Islam, Christianity (including Protestantism and Catholicism) and Taoism. Since the establishment of the People's Republic of China, the People's Government has attached great importance to safeguarding religious freedom, as is explicitly stated in the Constitution. All religions are equal in status. Each has its own organizations and carries on its own religious activities. Religious adherents are to enjoy normal religious life. The Christians in China have made significant progress in promoting in their churches self-government, self-support and self-propagation.

> As is well known, the vicious Gang of Four brought about serious damages in all fields, and religion was certainly not exempted. But in the brief period of less than three years since the downfall of the Gang of Four, rehabilitation and development in all fields of work in the country have been speedily going on. The People's Government is making every effort to implement its various policies. The policy of religious freedom is again being seriously implemented in accordance with constitutional stipulation. Now steps are being taken to resume religious activities in churches and temples in accordance with practical needs. Religious organizations are on the way of consolidation.

> We, believers of various religions, in obedience to our respective faiths, are confident that good will prevail against evil and peace will triumph over war. We resolve to go hand in hand with religious people in other countries in dedication to this sublime cause.

The speaker's qualifications, as communicated at the press conference, were impressive: Zhao is Acting President of the Buddhist Association of China, member of the National People's Congress of the PRC, member of the Standing Committee of the Chinese People's Political Consultative Conference, and Vice-Chairman of the China-Japan Friendship Association. No doubt, his voice as well as that of the other Chinese delegates to Princeton, carries loud and far with those in power.

d. The situation of _Islam_ is somewhat different from that
of the other religions. In 1950, there were 30 million
Muslims in China; now, according to the Muslim representat-
atives at Princeton, there are only 10 million. Many of them
are blond, blue-eyed Chinese living in Xinjiang a North-
Western province which has been the traditional Chinese
gateway to the West. Their privileged position is due to the
fact that they are treated more as a racial minority than
as an organized religion. (Bush:264-96) Hence,this favorable report from Mr Zhang Jie, of the Islamic Association
of China, as noted by Mr Nezu:

> The equality of all citizens and the freedom of religion
> have now become a reality. In regions where minorities
> live, a Committee for Minorities now functions. Muslims
> do not eat pork. Therefore, special canteens have been
> set up by the Muslim authorities and by the workers.
> Muslim customs are perfectly protected. Muslims are
> living a happy and harmonious life. They ardently love
> their great leader; they ardently love socialism.

The _BR_, 10/26, tells us that, on October 19, a delegation
of Muslims left Beijing for Mecca. It was led by none other
than Muhammed Ali Zhang Jie, Vice-president of the Islamic
Association of China. The _BR_ concludes: "This is the first
time a group of Chinese Muslims make a pilgrimage to Mecca
since 1964."

On December 20, Xinhua reports: "The Beijing Islamic Association was inaugurated at a ceremony today." The report
continues:

> "Imam Al-hajji Salah An Shiwei, who was elected chairman,
> called the founding of the Association "a happy event for
> Beijin's 160.000 Muslims" and "an expression of government
> policy of freedom of religious belief." He pledged himself
> to work to unite the city's Muslims to work for China's mo-
> dernization program."

e. _Christianity_ will be treated more extensively in the chap-
ters which follow. Briefly, this is what was said in
September at the occasion of the visit of a group of professors from Leuven University to the University of Beijing:

> The position of Christianity is different from that of
> any other religion. It was forcefully introduced to
> China on the decks of British and other men of war; it
> took advantage of exorbitant privileges wrested from
> the Chinese by the Unequal Treaties; it enjoyed extra-
> territoriality and the political protection of foreign
> powers. Hence, the Christian religions (Protestant and
> Catholic) became the enemies of the people. They are
> the symbols of the loss of Chinese sovereignty.

History tells us that this terrible indictment is not without serious grounds, and that there is good reason, on the part of Christianity, to regret certain events and attitudes of the past, and humbly to atone for them.

History does not easily forget and forgive. This thought should never leave us as we approach a new epoch in Church-and-China relations.

Beijing Review, No. 51

December 21, 1979

For Your Reference

Origin of Religions In China

IN China, there are Daoism, Buddhism, Christianity (including Catholicism, Protestantism and the Orthodox Eastern Church) and Islamism.

Daoism originated in ancient China when the Han people worshipped celestial beings and necromancers of the Qin and Han Dynasties sought an "elixir of life" and attempted to contact spirits. Daoism arose towards the end of the Eastern Han Dynasty in the second century.

Buddhism was introduced into China from India via Central Asia in the first century. It gradually mingled with Chinese thought and culture and after the Southern and Northern Dynasties (420-589), native Buddhist sects such as Tiantai and Chan Zong sects appeared in China, which later spread to Japan and other countries.

In areas inhabited by Mongolians and Tibetans, the dominant religion is Lamaism.

Both Daoism and Buddhism had had great influence in Chinese history. Many simultaneously believed in Buddhism and worshipped Daoist deities but most would not enter a temple to burn incense except in the hope of gaining something. It was impossible to know exactly how many were believers of these two religions.

In the mid-7th century, with the development of communications between the East and the West, Islamic Arabs and Persian merchants in turn arrived in China and built mosques. According to earliest related historical records, in 651, an Arab envoy appeared before the Tang Dynasty emperor and expounded the Islamic creed and Arab customs and habits. Historians consider that the year of 651 marked the introduction of Islamism to China.

Before liberation, in north and northwest China, most of the Huis, Uygurs, Kazakhs, Uzbeks, Tajiks, Tartars, Khalkhas, Salars and other minority peoples were followers of Islamism. There are nearly 10 million Moslems in China.

Some Christian religious sects found their way to China in the Tang Dynasty (618-907). They never became very widespread and subsequently vanished. In 1582, Catholicism was reintroduced to China by the Italian Jesuit missionary Matteo Ricci (1552-1610). It is believed that the Catholic cathedral near Xuanwumen, Beijing, was built by Matteo Ricci and another missionary named Johann Adam Schall von Ball (1591-1666) in the early 17th century.

But it was only in the last hundred years that Christianity was introduced into China in a big way. After the Opium War in 1840, many Catholic, Protestant and Orthodox Eastern Church missionaries played a despicable role serving imperialist and colonialist aggression against China. That provoked continuous resistance from the Chinese people against the imperialist missionaries, the most famous one being the Yi He Tuan (Boxer) Movement in 1900.

On the eve of liberation, there were about 3 million Catholics, 700,000 Protestants and a small following of the Orthodox Eastern Church in China.

6. Towards greater tolerance of religion?

I should like to give some elements of an answer to this important question. All Christians wish this answer could be an unconditional yes. Unfortunately such is not the case.

The official basis of religious freedom in the PRC is Article 46 of the Constitution, adopted by the Fifth National Congress of the People, March 5, 1978: "Citizens are free to believe in religion, free not to believe, and free to propagate atheism." The official French translation of this text has a somewhat different ring: "Les citoyens ont la liberté de pratiquer une religion, la liberté de ne pas pratiquer de religion et de propager l'athéisme." Apparently, in view of both translations, "to believe" is "to practice." Indeed, why freedom to believe if one is not allowed to practice? Or could the government also want control over the hidden thoughts of believers? Or worse still, by force of habit would the government want to continue, even after the downfall of the Gang of Four, "to hit the dog in the water"? 落水狗, which is Lu Xun's way of saying "don't take pity on a dangerous enemy."

Most observers feel that there is a new soft line in China's attitude toward religion. Others are sceptical, even cynical. As a friend puts is: "So many zigs have happened after so many zags the last three years that what's right today may be wrong tomorrow. Ideologically, the Chinese people are confused more than ever." Perhaps this is so. I for one feel that there are harbingers of hope, no doubt ambiguous, but real. On this matter, I'm willing to indulge in a guarded optimism and enjoy the benefit of the doubt. Here are some disjointed facts which feed my optimism.

-- On March 16, the Religious Affairs Bureau which had been dormant for years was resurrected. Xiao Xianfa, who headed the Bureau at the time of its demise in 1966 was again put in charge. On that day, the Central Committee of the Chinese Communist Party enumerated the merits of the Bureau: it united and educated the masses of believers, launched a Patriotic Movement to sever the ties between the Chinese churches and foreign imperialism, and promoted democratic reforms within religious institutions. (PD, March 19) The importance of the Bureau is evident if only for the reason that it depends directly from the Council of State.

-- In Kunming, capital of Yunnan province, a national-level conference was held from February 12 to 22. This conference decided on a six-year plan for academic research

in religion sponsored by the government. Janathan Chao
reports from Hong Kong:

> The aim of the Conference was to initiate a process of
> scholarly study on religions. This, of course, is also
> to be from the Marxist point of view, namely, dialecti-
> cal and historical materialism. But more particularly,
> the Chinese Marxist research interest is focused on
> three areas: 1. The emergence, development, and decline
> of various religions; 2. The history, present state,
> sectarian divisions, doctrinal beliefs and scriptures
> of each religion and the functional role religions play
> in social history; and 3. "Scientific atheism" and the
> policy of the proletariat toward religions. (Scherer:36)

-- The Kunming Conference also founded the "Chinese Society
for Religious Studies." The society has 56 council members. Zhao Puchu (see p. 74-5) is chairman while two
Christians, K.H. Ting and Zhao Fusan (see below) and
others, are vice-chairmen. (BR, 12/21:22)

-- In September 1978, the Institute for the Study of World
Religions was inaugurated. Zhao Fusan is its Deputy Director. The Institute has set up liaison with universities in Europe and America. It graciously receives a
stream of foreign visitors anxious to know the situation
of the Chinese religious world.(See below)

-- Lastly, in September 1979, Mr Xiao Xianfa, with whom we
are by now familiar, announced a slate of religious leaders recently elected to posts of great responsibility:

> More than twenty people from religious circles were
> elected deputies to the Fifth National People's Con-
> gress and members of the National Committee of the
> Chinese People's Political Consultative Conference.
> The prominent Tibetan, Banqen Erdini was elected vice-
> chairman of the CPPCC National Committee, Wu Yaozong,
> chairman of the Patriotic Movement Committee of the
> Protestant Churches in China, was elected member of
> the standing committee of the NPC; Burhan Shahidi,
> president of the Islamic Association of China, and
> Bishop Ding Guangxun were elected members of the
> National Standing Committe of the CPPCC, Zhang Jiashu,
> vice-president of the Chinese Patriotic Catholic As-
> sociation, the venerable Zheng Guo (p. 74), imam Al-
> Hadji an Shiwei (p. 76) and Bishop Yang Gaojian (see
> below) have also been elected to the 5th CPPCC Nation-
> al Committee.

These then are the government's men, and its official liturgists. I have taken this information from an article which appeared in the Ta Kung Pao, September 27, entitled "China's policies on religious freedom." The article is based on a Xinhua interview with Mr Xiao. In Xiao's own words, "Religious freedom is our Party's consistent policy."

Mr Xiao made much of the "renovation of monasteries." He said that, as part of the effort to follow Party policy on religion, some places have unfrozen rent that had been paid to local religious institutions and restored the wages of religious officials, in some cases giving back wages that had been held back from them. Xiao had precise details about famous places now again open to the public:

> Many religious centers in Xinjiang, Qinghai, Ningxia and Yunnan are now open to visitors and worshippers. Famous monasteries and places of worship now under renovation include Beijing's Yonghe Lamasery, Fa Yuansi (Temple of the Cource of Buddhist Teaching) and the mosque on Niujie street, Zhejiang province's Tiantong Temple and Asoka Monastery, Nanjing's Qixia Monastery, Guangzhou's Stone Room Cathedral and Shanghai's Xuhui Cathedral.

In sum, according to Mr Xiao:

> Catholic clergymen and monks in China are returning to their posts, religious institutions have resumed activities and famous monasteries and places of worship have been renovated and are being reopened to worshippers.

This may be a good beginning, but it is only a beginning of a movement that might bring true religious freedom to the Chinese people.

Finally, two matters call for more attention: the interpretation of constitutional freedom of religion, and the role of atheism in the PRC.

a. First, the interpretation of constitutional freedom:

Again, Mr Xiao Xienfa will be our authoritative guide, so much the more so that, what he has to say, was aimed at a Christian tourist group whom he met in Beijing, April 1979. Details of this interview have been revealed for the first time by Jonathan Chao. (Scherer:32)

Mr Xiao briefly described four periods of religious
policy as carried out by the Communist Party from
1935 to 1954. He omitted the fact that, from 1922 to
1927, and again from 1927 to 1943, the CCP systema-
tically persecuted the Christian church and laicized Buddhist monks. He then denounced the Gang of
Four and piloried their persecution of all religions
"under the pretext that religion did no longer exist
in China." Since the Civil War Period (1945-49)
and the Common Program Period (1949-54), the CCP has
implemented its "united front" policy for the purpose
of uniting minority ethnic and religious groups with
the Party in spite of their ideological differences.

Xiao was emphatic on this point: "This 'united front
policy' will be continued by the government so long
as there are religious people. It was so, it is so
now, and it will be so! Under the leadership of the
CCP, all the Chinese people, including religious
people, are pursuing the goals of socialist revolution and reconstruction. Now they are marching
toward the goal of the Four Modernizations."

Mr Xiao also added this prediction: "Religion will
not disappear until we have eliminated the exploitation of man by man, and until social productive
forces, science and technology will sufficiently be
developed. During the socialist period (which precedes the ideal, or communist, period) religion will
continue to exist because the social and ideological
factors on which it rests still are with us."

Mr Xiao then gave an interesting definition of religious
freedom which he put in nine points as follows:

1. One is free to believe and free not to believe religion.
2. One is free to choose one's religion.
3. One is free to believe today, and free not to believe tomorrow.
4. All religions, big or small, are equal; no religion
   shall occupy a position of dominance in China.
5. The political status of believers and non-believers
   is equal.
6. The government does not take administrative measures
   against the religions.
7. Religious believers are free to entertain friendly
   relations with believers in other continents.
8. Each religion can have its own administration, such
   as the Three-Self Patriotic Association, the Buddhist
   Association and the Muslim Association.
9. There is co-existence between believers and non-believers as they jointly pursue revolutionary goals
   and engage in socialist reconstruction.

Jonathan Chao remarks at this point that the CCP proclaims "freedom of religious belief" not because it sees any intrinsic value in religion or believes in the "inalienable right" of man to hold religious beliefs; instead, "freedom of religious belief" is a temporary lenience for enlisting religious people to participate in China's socialist reconstruction.

Chao further gives the following critical appreciation of Mr Xiao's nine points:

> The first three points deal with a person's inner movement away from faith or toward faith, a realm which can hardly be legislated. The fourth through sixth points deal with the legal position of religious persons under the Constitution, namely, that they are not culpable. But this legal status does not mention the rights of free assembly, of pursuing a religious career, or propagating the faith. But in the light of traditional Chinese state control of religion, freedom from guilt is already an extension of grace on the part of the state. The last three points deal with the role of religious people in overall "united front" policy toward social reconstruction. (Scherer:33)

In conclusion, one might say that, at present, to have "religious belief" is no longer a crime as was the case during the Cultural Revolution and under the Gang of Four. But this freedom should not be manifested publicly, and, in practice, religion should not be talked about or communicated in the privacy of the home. Only atheism enjoys this privilege. Yet, Christians should be grateful for small favors from the government: they are no longer public enemies and, of course, they are totally free to confess the faith in the intimacy of their hearts -- where the Lord sees and understands. (Proverbs, 24:12)

b. Second, the privileged role of atheism in the PRC:

There is no Communism without an active promotion of atheism, as Mr Xiao Xienfa has correctly explained. (p.66) To this iron rule, Mao's thought makes no exception. Chu Mei-fen, in her unpublished thesis The Religious Dimension of Mao Tsetung's Thought, Chicago University, 1977, p. 263-70, makes this pointed observation:

> Mao Tsetung Thought is atheistic and militantly so. The religious policy of China reflects the tension in Mao Tsetung Thought, namely, an active undermining of religious propaganda and belief, on the one hand, and a passive tolerance because of the awareness that no one can be coerced into believing or into not believing.

We have repeatedly seen that the latest official declarations stress the continuity of Mao's policy, a fact which burst upon the religious scene at the occasion of the China Atheism Seminar, held at Nanjing, December 10-19, 1978.

The first details about this Seminar came out in the Ta Kung Pao, December 31, 1978. They were followed by a comprehensive report in the Guang-ming Ribao, January 6, 1979, and presented in a more scientific way in the February issue of Zhexue Yanjiu, Philosophical Studies. The full English text of the Guang-ming Ribao, from which I borrow the following quotation, was prepared by the China Liaison Office of the United Methodist Church in Hong Kong. I also draw upon Jonathan Chao's account in Scherer, p. 36.

> The Nanjing Seminary on Atheism was jointly sponsored by the new Institute of World Religions of the Academy of Social Sciences and the Philosophy Department of Nanjing University ("an institution originally founded by Protestant missionaries to spread Christian theism," as Chao puts it).

> The forty participants agreed that religion still has an influence, also in China. The struggle against theism retains its actuality: it will lead to spiritual liberation and thereby contribute to the Four Modernizations. It was resolved at the end of the Seminar to set up a "Chinese Society for the Study of Atheism," with temporary headquarters in the Philosophy Department of the University of Nanjing. The study of atheism, delegates felt, provides a solid foundation for the study of Chinese thought, the history of Chinese philosophy and the background of peasant struggles.

+
+ +

Perhaps the attentive reader thinks that the above texts are characterized by boring repetition. Yet, I felt they should be mentioned with the benefit of context better to enable the reader to get "the feel" of words constantly on the lips of high officials referring to religion in the PRC. Indeed, the correct interpretation of words (as Confucius said long ago) is the gateway to the correct interpretation of action. Or as Mao would say: "Only practice counts."

In brief, this much can now be said: While , on the one hand, there are signs of a religious thaw, there are, on the other hand, also renewed vexations heaped upon religious people less anxious to toe the official line. I have heard from several sources, including Bishop Ting, that the scrapping from Article 46 of the Constitution the clause that discriminates in favor of atheism remains a distinct possibility. But I also have heard from one of the Leuven professors who went to China in September that their learned interlocutors from the University of Beijing were emphatic: "We don't want this clause to be touched; we want to remain an atheistic state."

Therefore, unless I see proof to the contrary, I feel that it is safe to conclude that little if anything has changed since the fall of the Gang of Four, and that the remolding process for many believers goes on with unabated vigor. It is common knowledge that this process has a fourfold objective:

1. To extirpate all feudalistic and, in the case of Christians, all imperialistic thought.

2. To develop socialist idealism and love of country through the banishment of all foreign religious influences unless they unconditionally submit to government directives.

3. To eliminate those religious practices which might escape the Party's control.

4. To have whatever is left of religion conform to communist ideology so as to hasten its early disappearance.

The reaction to these goals by believers in general, and particularly by Christians, has varied according to time and place; neither is there a uniform application of that repressive tolerance which our texts imply. Some believers have tried to accommodate the government, such as members of the Three-Self Movement on the Protestant, and of the Patriotic Church on the Catholic, side. In their case, there is a tendency to play down the other-worldly, dogmatic, and institutional requirements of their faith. But these requirements, to other Chinese Christians, are so basic that they prefer to suffer, even unto death, rather than abandoning them. For all I know, there is acknowledged good faith on either side. But the gap that separates both groups is real and deep, perhaps beyond the point of reconciliation.

Whether, at the end of the dark tunnel through which Chinese Christians now travel, the ideal communist state will wait for them, that is an open question.

Chapter 3:

Protestants respond to the new situation

Literature on present-day Christianity in China is more abundant on Protestant than on Catholic side, witness the four pages of bibliographical references in IDOC, 12:29-32. Even though much of the information which we have cannot meet the test of scientific verification, we are reasonably well informed about the main trend of religious events in the PRC. In interpreting the information which we read, it will be necessary to take into account the confessional background of the informant. The data which follow have been selected from a mass of news items for reason of their specific interest to Catholic readers.

Donald MacInnis, Director of the Midwest China Study Resource Center, St. Paul, Minnesota, has contributed an excellent article to the 1979 Concilium issue on China, entitled "The Churches in New China." He briefly outlines the antecedents of the present situation. It is important to remember, also for Catholic purposes, that the first stage in reorganisation of the churches was to implement the "three-self" model, first articulated in the Christian Manifesto of May 1950, signed by 400,000 Protestant Christians: self-support, self-propagation and self-government.

The second stage, the merging of Protestant denominational efforts into a single organisation, began with the Three-Self Reform Movement, initiated by 151 church leaders at a meeting in Peking in April 1951 called by Premier Zhou Enlai. In the United Declaration of Chinese Christian Churches, the conference delegates called upon Chinese Christians "... to thoroughly, permanently and completely sever all relations with American missions and all other missions, thus realising self-government, self-support and self-propagation in the Chinese church. They also pledged to support the government's land reform policy, the Common Program, to obey all laws, to exert every effort in reconstruction of the nation, and "to assist the government to discover and punish antirevolutionary and corrupt elements within the Protestant church."

The standard accusations against Christianity often heard today are far from new. They have been epitomized in a message which nineteen Protestant church leaders in December 1949, a few days after Mao proclaimed the People's Republic of China, sent to mission boards abroad.

There does exist some deep-rooted feeling on the part of the Communists that the Christian church has been intimately related to imperialism and capitalism. It is a fact that the Christian church in China in the past has been entangled with the Unequal Treaties imposed upon China under duress; it did enjoy certain special privileges accruing from them... There were also close connections with the churches abroad in personnel and financial support. It modeled after the patterns in Britain and America... The Christian movement will have its due place in the future Chinese society and will have a genuine contribution to make. Its future will not emerge through this historical change unaffected. It will suffer a purge, and many of the withered branches will be amputated. But we believe it will emerge stronger and purer in quality, a more fitting witness to the gospel of Christ.

This quotation is found in Documents of the Three-Self Movement, New York: Asia Department, NCCCUSA, 1963, p. 151. It sets a pattern of recriminations against Protestant Christianity which is still repeated by the present leaders of the Three-Self Movement, such as Bishop K.H. Ting whose 1974 address I quote below. The very expression of these grievances remains vital to an understanding of our ecumenical relations in China and abroad. (Bush: 170-263)

It is fitting to recall here the name of Wu Yaozong, already mentioned on p. 79. Y.T. Wu, as he is better known in foreign circles, was chairman of the Chinese Protestant Patriotic Three-Self Movement; he died in Shanghai on September 9th at the age of 86.

His funeral was attended by leading public personalities. According to the New China Press (Shanghai), vice-chairman Chang of the Shanghai revolutionary committee, in his speech of condolence, noted that "in 1950 under the guidance and instruction of Chairman Mao and Premier Chou, Wu Yao-tsung created the Protestant Self-Three Patriotic Movement. He united the masses of believers in love of the new China to follow the socialist way and assisted the government to implement the policy of religious freedom. He participated actively in international meetings to foster Chinese friendship with other peoples, and make a contribution to anti-imperialism, anti-colonialism and the cause of world peace. (IL, 12:3)

It is well known that the Bureau of Religious Affairs
was and remains the directing hand behind the Three-Self
Movement -- as well as behind the National Patriotic
Catholic Association which was formed in 1957 with the late
Archbishop Pi Shushi as chairman. The Bureau, of which
the past and present director is Mr Xiao Xianfa, whom we
have heard at length, bestirred itself to set up Christian
groups one against the other, and Chinese Christians against
their foreign brethren.

What of the future of the Three-Self Movement? Let me
quote a carefully formulated prognostic by Arne Sovik,
director of the Department of Studies, The Lutheran World
Federation, Geneva:

> The Three-Self Movement is likely to have some diffi-
> culty in functioning as a national church body, for if
> reports that have come to Hong Kong are at all indica-
> tive of the mind of the Protestants who have lived
> through these last.difficult years, the Movement lacks
> the confidence of many if not most local groups, which
> tend to see it as a political rather than a religious
> instrument. The tension that is the heritage of accus-
> ation meetings of the early 1950's, and of the differ-
> ences between the "faithful" and the Christians who
> compromised or left the faith during the Cultural Revol-
> ution period has already created a problem reminiscent
> of the Donatist controversy. As long as these memories
> last there is likely to be either great reluctance to
> develop a unified Protestantism or a tendency toward
> something analogous to the Baptist churches of the
> Soviet Union, where unrecognized groups live in inse-
> curity and some suspicion of the recognized church
> which has accepted government registration. If in the
> last generation the western denominational differences
> have broken down, there seems to be evidence of a threat
> of other divisions, the result of theological differ-
> ences to be sure, but also of different responses to
> the problem of life in socialist China.(Scherer:29)

As will be evident from the pages which follow, the par-
allelism of the Protestant and the Catholic religious situation as described by Dr Sovik is a silent invitation for
all Christians, be it in China or in the Church at large,
to band forces toward the solution of a common problem.

During the last several months, many Protestants have
visited the Chinese continent, either in group or alone.
These contacts have brought us fresh information which
Catholics are anxious to digest. Here are some points
worthy of note:

1. <u>John Curnow</u>, a Catholic priest from New Zealand, went to
China with a Christian group in October 1978. During
his 18-days trip, he visited five cities in the East and
had a close exposure to rural China where 700 million of
the total population live. I quote from his mimeographed
report:

> As a Christian group we had established as one of our
> goals to make contact with the Church and with Christi-
> ans in China. Our guides and interpreters knew little
> about religion and could not offer much hope. They
> also seemed to make little distinction between religi-
> ons, regarding Christianity, Taoism, Islam and Buddhism
> in much the same way. We had made two definite requests:
> one, to meet Anglican Bishop K.H. Ting whose name was
> known through his international work with the Christian
> Student Movement and the World Council of Churches. It
> had also been reported that he had attended the recent
> 5th People's Congress along with some other religious
> leaders. He was known to be on the Stadning Committe
> of the People's Political Consultative Conference, an
> organisation that brings together all elements in
> Chinese society, including representatives of religion,
> as well as those who belong to the communist Party.
>
> The present policy is not to emphasise differences but
> to seek common ground, a common front. This does not
> mean that the government favors religion but it needs
> the support of all the people, including religious
> people to build socialism. Most Christians, we were
> told, believing that the new China is better than the
> old, work for this common goal. We were able to meet
> Bishop Ting.
>
> Among the Protestants, the multitude of denominations
> has gone. Christians of all kinds meet together.
> There is no wish to reintroduce denominations. The
> Chinese Protestant Christians hope to work through
> their situation without interference from the West and
> are opposed to those movements which are trying to get
> back into China at this stage with missionary models
> that are not suitable.

It will be remarked that, although Curnow's last paragraph does not mention Bishop Ting by name, the ideas are
his. Ting has consistently opposed the return of missionaries.

2. <u>Marjorie and Cyril</u> Powles are Anglicans from Canada
and dear personal friends. They visited China, from
Beijing to Gwangzou, between March 23 and April 11, 1979.
They published a short account of their trip in <u>The Japan
Christian Quarterly</u>, Fall, 1979, p. 249, from which I lift
the details which follow:

For us the highlight of the trip was a full day visit
with Professor Ding Guangxun and his wife, Professor
Guo Siumai, known to their many friends in the West
as K.H. and Siu May Ting... Today, after many vicissi-
tudes, it can be said that the Christian movement in
China has justified its own right to exist. Chinese
Christians have participated actively in the struggle
toward socialism, which they interpreted as God's liberating act. In contrast to their former isolation
from one another, Catholics and Protestants are joining
with Buddhists, Muslims, and others to form an association of religious bodies.

The Nanjing Theological College, whose principal K.H.
Ting was, has now been transformed into a center for
religilus studies at Nanjing University, with Ting as
its director. Chinese Protestants are carrying out a
new translation of the Bible into contemporary Chinese
and will have government support for its publication.

Finally, church buildings confiscated during the Cultural Revolution will be renovated and returned for use
by their original owners.

The problems raised for Roman Catholics when they elected bishops without Vatican sanction have been widely
publicized. Protestants have gone even further in a
radical "de-institutionalization" of their church bo
dies. The old denominational distinctions have vanished,
together with hierarchical and territorial structures
like bishops and dioceses. (Ting was formerly Anglican
bishop of Shanghai.) House meetings stress Bible study,
prayer, and a simple breaking of bread. The Church as
Movement (People of God) seems more evident today in
China than the Church as Institution (Body of Christ).

Dr. and Mrs. Ting spoke of many plans for the future,
now that the oppressive Gang of Four are gone and the
nation has returned to a proper recognition of religious freedom.

Obviously, this is a factual report on what the Powles
heard from the Tings. Cyril Powles is a good theologian
and a good Anglican priest whom I have known for many
years in Tokyo. I regret that he did not add his personal
reflections about the new kind of Christianity described
by Bishop Ting.

. A group of twenty-two Hong Kong pastors visited China
from March 21 to April 7, 1979. This was the first Chi-
ese Protestant tour group since 1949. It was, indeed, a
istoric event as they in the sights at Hangzhou, Shanghai,
anjing and Beijing, and were given splendid receptions by

representatives of the Three-Self Patriotic Movement, officials in the United Front Work Department, and senior cad-
res of the Religious Affairs Bureau in these cities. Peter
K.L. Lee, director of the Christian Study Center on Chinese
Religion and Culture at Tao Fong Shan, Hong Kong, reports
on this trip in Ching Feng, No. 2, 1979, p. 57-74.

We soon learned that most of the ones who came to see
us (at Guangzhou Railway Station) have held positions
in the provincial or municipal committees of the China
Three-Self Patriotic Movement which came into being in
the early 1950's and which since then has been the officially recognized spokesmen for Protestantism in
China. One of those who spoke condemned the Gang of
Four for a great deal of destruction and suffering, in
which Christians had their share, and they said that not
until now did they dare to come out openly as Christians.

Following the service, a group discussion was held. One
question had to do with evangelism in China today. The
answer was given that mass evangelism in public places
is not appropriate, not because it is against any laws
but it may lead to a public disturbance in case heated
argument with atheists ensues. Person-to-person evangelism is certainly possible... It is true that the
      present China is built on a thoroughly secular
ideology. But the remarkable thing is that, at this
moment at least, freedom of religion is guaranteed...
In recent years in China, a hard demarcation has been
drawn between what is considered to be official Christianity, as represented by the Three-Self Movement, and
those who do not go along with it. I know too well
that this is the picture which many Hong Kong Chinese
Christians as well as some western missionaries have
of Christianity in China today. The Three-Self people
I talked to at first declined to have much to say about
those Christians who want to have nothing to do with
them.

In Nanjing, K.H. Ting was there and spoke first. He
said something about Christianity being deinstitutionalized and declericalized in China today... I know
that the fundamentalist preacher Wang Ming-tao was
vehemently opposed to Ting along with others whom he
called modernists. Wang's opinion has had a large
influence on the conservative Chinese Christian views
of Ting and the Three-Self Movement. But from my personal contact this time I cannot believe that all of
the people who are willing to lend themselves be group-
ed under the name of the Three-Self Patriotic Movement
have betrayed the Gospel. Earnestly I hope that whatever breach there may have been among the Chinese

Christians will be healed. I feel very strongly that those from the outside must not make the breach harder to overcome. If we do, we are doing the Christian cause a disservice.

What Peter Lee says deserves careful consideration. I want to join him enthusiastically in his hope that the rift between Chinese Christians will be healed. And I fully agree: the initiative will have to come from themselves.

4. Andrew K.H. Hsiao, who is principal of the Lutheran Theological Seminary in Hong Kong, visited China in June-July. Here are parts of his report from Information Letter, No. 26, October 1979:

I asked the church leaders: "Is there any change in the Chinese Communist religious policy?" They replied: "The policy of the Chinese Communists is freedom of religion. The policy itself has not changed. If there is any change it lies in the implementation of the policy."

As one church leader remarked: "Our government now knows that the freedom of religion is the right of the people that cannot be suppressed by force." ... The Chinese church has been transformed from a "visible" to an "invisible" church, from an institutional to a non-institutional church (Bishop Ting calls it the "deinstitutionalized church), from a "public" to a "household" church, from a church of the lips to a church of the heart...

I cannot be concerned that the alleged antagonism between both groups (those associated with the Christian Three-Self Patriotic Movement and those belonging to the "household churches") may prove harmful for the re-awakening of the very weak Chinese church. The Chinese church needs different kinds of people. She needs those who live behind closed doors, praying and reading their Bibles and she needs also those who publish Bibles and build churches. Bishop Ting believes that both the "household churches" and the more visible churches will both exist in the future. And with a smile he said to me: "I will attend both."

On the atmosphere in which these conversations took place (seven hours with Chao Fusan, about whom see the next chapter, and nine hours with Bishop Ting), Dr Hsiao reports:

Generally speaking, all the discussions were carried out in a very open, sincere and calm atmosphere. There were exceptions of course. When discussing the religious policy of the Chinese communists, some persons uncontrollably repeated the communist line. Others, when questioned on the future of the Chinese Church, were evasive and began to "shadow box" instead of speaking to the point. Still others, when reminded of the suffering because of their faith, were overcome by emotion and broke into tears. (Ching Feng, 3:133)

Dr Hsiao is a good observer, and a good psychologist. There is one question which he does not answer: Do we have a modicum of data which would allow us to judge the situation also from the viewpoint of Christian doctrine and tradition?

5. Jonathan Chao. The last 1979 Protestant visitor to China whom I shall introduce is the Rev. Jonathan Chao, director of the Chinese Church Research Center in the China Graduate School of Theology, Hong Kong. He is co-editor of China and the Church Today. Together with his wife, Chao spent the month of September in China. The report from which I quote is found in his publication, September-December 1979.

THE CHRISTIAN CHURCHES IN CHINA

On the eve of the proclamation of the People's Democratic Republic of China, 1 October 1949, the Christian communities in China counted about 4.000.000 members. Statistics give the following numbers:

Roman Catholics: 3.275.000 with 146 bishops (111 foreign, 35 Chinese), 5.788 priests (2.090 foreign, 2.698 Chinese). The Catholic Church owned 3 universities, 189 secondary schools and 2.011 primary schools with a total of 567.732 students.

The Protestant denominations numbered 750.000 believers (Church of Christ in China: 177.000, True Jesus Church: 125.000, China Inland Mission, 85.000, Anglicans: 77.000, Lutherans: 65.000, Methodists: 147.000, Baptists: 81.000).

The churches directed 13 universities, 240 secondary schools, 44 theological institutes, and 21 Bible schools.

IDOC, December 1979

Sino-American normalization has created a great change within China not only for the good of those having relatives in America and for scientific and technological exchanges, but also for giving much hope to the population in general, who expect to in some way benefit concretely from this restored relationship...

On September 16, we attended the Catholic service in Peking, with nearly a thousand Chinese filling the old cathedral. On September 23, we attended the two newly opened Protestant churches in Shanghai. The Moore Memorial Church has about 1200, both young and old.

China is a multidimensional reality that must be experienced. The art of survival, the influence of human relations, the contest of wits, the conflicting desires for human fulfillment, and the quest for inner values and peace are all at work within the framework of Marxist society. But that society is still dominated by Confucian values. The old problem is still there. How can anyone solve the problem of traditional Chinese selfishness by "modernization?"

Elsewhere in the same issue, Jonathan Chao describes the "house church meetings" which have drawn much attention in Protestant news from China. He says that Christians in China have learned to be "wise as serpents and gentle as doves." They have learned to share their Christian faith with their immediate family members or extended family members. "Likewise, they introduce the Gospel to their trusted friends. The approach insures that they will not be betrayed by those to whom they preach the Gospel."

Chao also found examples of signal Christian charity, particularly in the care of the families of Christian brothers who have been arrested and imprisoned for many years. He tells us that:

Those who suffered for Christ in China during the last thirty years are too numerous to count. Their courage to stand up for their faith and their willingness to go through sustained suffering have been an open testimony of their loyalty to Christ, a testimony that lives on in the memories of those who witnessed their suffering. After suffering from betrayals at the hands of less faithful believers, Christians have learned to protect each other against false brethren as well as against government investigators.

Jonathan Chao reports miracles and signs, such as cures
of terminal diseases. He then turns to the "limitations
of Christian life in China." There are four:

> Christians are often deprived of sacramental bles-
> sings; they are deprived of doctrinal instruc-
> tion; they are deprived of fellowship with outside
> believers in other parts of China and in the world;
> they are deprived of the opportunity for vocal pro-
> clamation of the Gospel and of Christian truth.

I felt deeply moved by Jonathan Chao's account. I know
him well, and he is dear to me for his obvious zeal and
sincerity. Much of what he said, as will be seen in the
pages which follow, also applies to the Catholic Church.

+
+ +

Let me finish with a reflection of the noted Protestant
theologian Lukas Vischer, of the World Council of Churches,
sent in at the occasion of a consultation in preparation of
the 1979 China issue of Concilium, edited by Claude Geffré
and myself, the title of which is China as a Challenge to
the Church.
Dr Vischer remarks: "China challenges the Church, but
what about the Church challenging China? I think that it is
here that we should raise theological questions or critique

BEIJING CHURCH HOLDS CHRISTMAS EVE SERVICE

Beijing, December 24. (Xinhua) -- Beijing's Protestant
church in the eastern part of the city resounded with
the singing and music of Christmas carols this evening at a Christmas Eve service attended by more than
200 Chinese and foreign Christians.

The service lasted more than an hour. Early tomorrow
morning, the Church will hold a communion service, followed by the regular Christmas service.

Before and after this evening's service, the Christians
exchanged festival greetings in front of two Christmas
trees twinklingwith color lights.

Xinhua learned that the newly-consecrated bishop Michael
Fu Tieshan will preside at mignight Mass in the city's
southern Catholic cathedral.

---

concerning human rights, political structures of communist
polity, interpretation of the meaning of power struggle
which is a permanent feature of that polity, or the meaning
of the freedom of the human spirit... This seems to me
possible if the authors will ask what are the costs to China
of its admittedly positive aspects in values and practice."

This brings up the question of balance in reporting on China; in establishing Christian communion with China; in trying to be of help. One of the most difficult things for us,
who live in a free and consumerist society, is fully to realize that the basic question for millions of Chinese is
their struggle for bread and justice. First bread, then
justice. And this also applies to the Chinese religions, and
to Christianity. It is their very survival which is at
stake.

Hence, I submit that, at this moment, all judgment is premature, and risks to be unfair and uncharitable. I also
submit that the Chinese people -- and the Chinese Christians,
be they of the "house churches" or of the Three-Self Movement
-- will in the long run know to distinguish between their
friends and their enemies, whether they come to them under
the banner of Mao or under the sign of the Cross.

INDEMNITY SOUGHT FOR PROPERTY IN CHINA

As reported in the April 23 issue of Missouri in Perspective, "the Lutheran Church-Missouri Synod is one of about
fifteen American denominations that plans to seek reimbursement from mainland China for mission properties confiscated by the communists in 1949."

Other Christian denominations, including the United Pres-
byterian Church, have declined to seek reimbursement feeling the Chinese may interpret the effort as hostile.

Reimbursement is now possible due to the normalization of
diplomatic relations between the U.S. and the People's
Republic of China. The formula for reimbursement is 41
cents on each dollar of property according to 1949 values.

The Chinese government has agreed to pay a total of $80.4
million dollars for properties taken, roughly $19.4 mil-
lion to American missionary and educational groups.

Asia Lutheran News, July 1979

AN EVALUATION OF THE COMMUNIST ATTITUDE TOWARDS CHRISTIANITY

If after nineteen years of stringent measures acted on in all the glow of revolution, Christianity has not only survived but has emerged with a nucleus of unshakable faithful, the second-generation Chinese, tired of slogans and endless political meetings, might be won over in considerable numbers by dedicated lay Chinese Christians.

The gospel which they have is their own gospel, not inherited from a western-financed foreigner with western-oriented ideas. The church which they form is a Chinese church, forged in the fires of persecution before God and man, and no longer a pale, weak shadow. The vision which the members share is a real and living thing for the dangerous and difficult present and not just a pie-in-the-sky opiate. They are the truly free men and women in a country rapidly losing the excitement of promised new freedoms in empty slogans and bondage.

George N. Patterson, Christianity in Communist China, p. 137

THE INCULTURATION OF CHRISTIANITY

Communism has another merit which makes it the way prepared by God for announcing the Gospel in China when the opportune moment will arrive. It is that the Church will dispense with all those activities which gave it a western aspect in China: schools, hospitals, universities, etc.

The Church could not give up these institutions because they were her chosen means to show the Chinese people Christ's charity. However, in operating them, the missionaries could have mistakenly let them appear means of proselytism or even propaganda for western culture.

Furthermore, these works were supported with money from Christian countries and, at times, from the colonial powers who obviously were not disinterested in their "charity." Thus the missions with all their plants appeared or could have appeared in a false or repugnant light to the Chinese.

Domenico Grasso, S.J., in Chu, p. 118

Chapter 4:

Zhao Fusan and the Institute for the Study of World Religions

Two Christians from China stood in the limelight of church news during 1979: Zhao Fusan and Ding Guangxun. Both are Anglicans; both visited the West during the year. Both occupy positions of great responsibility. Without necessarily speaking for the government, both have access to high administrative circles, and it is safe to say that the way they see things reflects fairly correctly the attitudes of the government toward Christianity. Hence, it is important to have a closer look at their persons and their work.

Mr Zhao is Deputy Director of the Research Institute on World Religions (RIWR) under the Chinese Academy of Social Sciences in Beijing. Zhao's great-grandfather and grandfather on his mother's side were Christian ministers. He was ordained in the Sheng Kong Hui, the Chinese Anglican-Episcopalian Church. For some time, he served as assistant to the Anglican bishop of North China. He was also Dean of Studies at the Yenching Union Theological Seminary in Beijing. During the Cultural Revolution he was sent away for re-education.

Zhao visited the United States in April-May as a member of the twelve-man delegation from his Academy. I had the privilege of meeting him personally on May 4, 1979, at the Divinity School of the University of Chicago. The occasion was the opening session of the Midwest China Consultation, the proceedings of which were edited by James A. Scherer under the title Western Christianity and the People's Republic of China: Exploring New Possibilities, 1979.

As I set next to him, and later at lunch, Mr Zhao questioned me on SODEPAX, the Vatican-WCC Joint Committee on Society, Development and Peace, of which I have been General Secretary. The subject must be of special interest to him as he brought it up again in a conversation with a mutual friend, Father Angelo Lazzarotto, in November, and this time in his own Institute.

Mr Zhao is at present totally committed to the work of the
Institute which is situated in a popular neighborhood of the
capital. The building is unassuming and makes the impression
of a refurbished factory. The Institute's director is Ren
Jiyu, a Buddhist scholar. There are 80 associates engaged
in scientific work related to Chinese Buddhism, Taoism, Christianity, Islam, western religion, and atheism, both Chinese
and foreign.

The Institute was established in 1964 with Mao's backing.
The avowed purpose was to study religion from a Marxist
point of view and in the service of proletarian politics.
It was inactivated under the pressure of the Gang of Four
and reopened again in September 1978. Unlike the Religious
Study Institute at the Nanjing University under K.H. Ting,
which is an educational facility, the Beijing Institute is
dedicated to the secular research in religion as a social
science. Work has begun on a dictionary of religious terms,
on the investigation of religious customs, particularly
among the Minorities, and on the collating and re-editing of
sacred scriptures, particularly those of Tibetan Buddhism.

During his American visit, Mr Zhao was very articulate
about the antecedents which account for Christianity's
predicament in China today. He freely distributed copies

MAO ON STUDYING RELIGION AND CRITICIZING THEOLOGY

In 1963 when Comrade Mao Zedong in a written instruction
commented on the importance of studying religion and criticizing theology, he concretely pointed out that, without criticizing theology, one cannot write good history
of philosophy, also cannot write good world history and
literary history.

This judgment cuts deeply. Historically religion wiel-
ded tremendous influence in the various aspects of social life, so that various social classes frequently
use it as a weapon in class struggle. Throughout history there were many class struggles which could not be
separated from religion, which even directly appeared
as the struggle between various religions or different
denominations, while sometimes appearing as the struggle
between religion and various atheistic currents of thinking.

Ren Jiyu, director, RIWR, <u>Ching Feng</u>, 22:85

of an important paper which he had prepared for western audiences. This paper received wide circulation, and it is found at the end of Scherer's book. Comments to the paper appeared in CN, 73:80-4. There is a fine German translation by Bernward Willeke, O.S.F., and others, which can be obtained at the Institute for Missiology, the University of Würzburg. It is hoped that the reader will have the occasion to read Mr Zhao's paper of which I quote here the last paragraph which aptly summarizes his thought:

> Our friends all over the world, including religious adherents in many lands, have closely followed over the last thirty years the development in China and introduced to their friends what achievements China had made. They are also willing to help us in realizing our goal. They are real friends of the Chinese people. Today, a growing number of Catholics and Protestants in the West have come to realize that any attempt at influencing China's progress with Christian missions would be futile as well as detrimental to the development of friendship with the Chinese people. On the other hand, there are still a few missionaries that are not happy with the socialist construction of China. They think they see a chance in the fall of Lin Biao and the Gang of Four to pick up again the road taken by the China missionaries long before them.

> In fact, the history of the last 100 years, especially the experience since the May 4 Movement, should have made plain the right answer. We are convinced, Christiand of the West would become good friends of the Chinese people if they would only know more about the history and interplay between the Chinese revolution and the foreign missions over the past one and one-half centuries and the present tasks of the Chinese people, and if they would work for the friendship and cultural interflow between the people of China and of various countries.

Mr Zhao, in the many interviews which he gave, answered a number of important questions. A choice of these questions here follows:

-- On Marxism in China: "While Marxism has been a different world view from religion, this does not mean in China that Christians cannot work with Marxists. It was said that you do not have to get agreement about believing in God before you can work together for the building of the society. Neither does it mean that Christians have to give up their faith in God in order to be part of a united front. This protection of religious freedom is stated in the Constitution of China and has been restated by the new leadership."(Curnow report, p. 4)

-- On Christian faith and Marxism: "It has been difficult
for Protestants and Roman Catholics and others (but especially for Protestants) to see the relationship of
Christian faith to socialist society. However, that
China with over 900 million people can feed itself and
provide a stable livelihood in quite an achievement,
only achieved through the socialist system... What holds
the country together? I slowly came to realize that Mao
Thought -- the revolutionary theory of socialism combin-
ed with Chinese reality -- is the only thing that unifies
us. No single religion could bring unity. Only socialism in a Chinese way could unify China, our dream for
years." (IL, 6:18-9)

-- On missionary activities: "I think that any premature
pressure to come in from the outside to search out
Christian groups or to seek opportunities for evangel-
izing activities, would be counter-productive and perhaps
embarrassing to the very people we would want least to
harm." (Mission Forum: 43)

"Churches and religious bodies should move slowly in offers of assistance. They must first make clear that
there will be no resumption of the old type of Christian
mission. The possibility of Christian missionaries en-
tering China for expressly evangelistic purposes is nil."
(CN, 61:70)

-- On priestly training: "I feel that Christians could learn
from the Buddhist way of educating young people to the
priesthood. Buddhists have the apprentice system whereby
an old monk teaches a young monk. Candidates to the
priesthood could be staying with elderly priests and
learn from them." (Chicago conversation)

-- On the ideals of Chinese youth: "To serve the people
wholeheartedly has become a common moral ideal for our
people. They courageously break away with idol worshipping and persist in finding truth from facts. They are
deeply concerned with world affairs and are ready to
learn everything advanced from foreign countries. These
spiritual features are easily found among the younger
generation. They are people with a new spirit cultiva-
ted by China's socialist system under the guidance of
Marxism-Leninism-Mao Zedong Thought. They are the hope
of our nation. (Scherer:78)

Mr Zhao made a deep impression on all of us at Chicago. I
feel that the decision to establish the Research Institute
on World Religions within the Academy of Social Sciences was
a bold one to take for the authorities, reversing a more
hostile, even radical, stand as advocated by the Gang of

Four. The very existence of the Research Institute is a challenge which, somewhat generally, I would put like this: "Can Christians prove to the satisfaction of the Institute in Beijing that Christianity has a real contribution to make to the welfare and the happiness of the Chinese people?" If we could do just that, we would find in Mr Zhao Fusan an able advocate, ready to pass on the good word to higher places where it really counts.

I vividly recall some remarks which Mr Zhao made while with us in Chicago. He hoped for greater contact with Christians in the West, particularly at an official, person-to-person basis, and not in groups. He stressed that the leaders of the Three-Self Movement will need from 3 to 5 years to recondition the churches, "at Chinese expense." He announced a new translation of the Bible being prepared in the current language, with simplified characters reading from left to right. And he finished telling me with a twinkle in his eyes: "Try to go slow! Try to be patient! And come when we are ready!"

I hope to meet Mr Zhao Fusan at the East-West Religions in Encounter Conference at Honolulu, June 16-27, 1980, which he serves as a resource person. The theme is "Buddhist-Christian Renewal and the Future of Humanity," a theme with which, I am sure, Mr Zhao feels quite at home.

DIALOGUE WITH ASIAN RELIGIONS AND TRADITIONS

God makes Himself known in many ways. There is a continuous revelation of God in the world, acting and healing, making whole and saving, creating man and transforming him, and calling us to discipleship. This is true not only of different political systems, but also of the great religions and ethical traditions of Asia, be they Buddhism, Taoism or Confucianism. These are also calling forth from us a critical involvement, a willingness to study and encounter these great influences in the lives of the people of Asia, in particular China. China itself has recently reopened the Institute of World Religions in Peking. Let's hope that an open dialogue will get started soon.

Just last November the Federation of Asian Bishops' Conferences stated: "Sustained and reflective dialogue with those who belong to other religions and even communion with them in prayer ... will reveal to us what the Holy Spirit has taught others to express in a marvelous variety of ways."

John Cioppa, M.M., in Mission Forum, p. 19.

Chapter 5:

Bishop Ting visits America

The second important visitor to the West was Bishop Ding
Guangxun, better known as K.H. Ting. Bishop Ting is at present Vice-chancellor of Nanjing University and Director of
the University's Institute of Religious Studies. He is a
member of the Chinese People's Political Consultative Conference, Vice-president of the Protestant Three-Self Movement, and, some predict, its future president in succession
to Wu Yaozong who died in September.

In 1966, Dr Ting was removed from his house when the Nanjing Theological Seminary was abruptly closed. Mr Ting, 64,
insists that he is "a former Anglican bishop, because the
Chinese now eschew such titles." He considers, however, that
he is still a bishop, although he no longer has an episcopal
role. Xinghua News Agency calls him "Bishop." He was the
Anglican bishop of Shanghai and Zhejiang.

Bishop Ting was deputy-leader of a group of Chinese religious leaders who attended the nine-day Third World Conference on Religion and Peace (WCRP), August 28 to September 7,
at Princeton University. The group included two Buddhists,
two Muslims, and four Christians: Han Wenzao, Deputy Secretary General of the Jiangsu Provincial Committee, Chen Zemin,
Dean of Nanjing Theological College, Li Shoupao, Associate
General Secretary of the National Committee for YMCA's in
China, and Bishop Ting who served as delegation leader and
spokesperson. This was only the second time in three deca-
des that any Chinese Christian leaders had been allowed to
visit the U.S.A. Understandably the group attracted wide attention, and was welcomed everywhere.

The question has been asked: "Why no Chinese Catholics at
Princeton?" Any answer must remain pure conjecture for an
outsider like myself. I imagine that the government, to balance the Protestant delegation may have thought of sending
an outstanding Catholic personality, such as Bishop-elect
Fu Tieshan, or Patriotic Church General Secretary Tang Lidao.

But there may have been misgivings on that score: how
would the media treat them once abroad? Or again, the
government might have considered Bishop Kong Pingmei, if he
is still alive and about. (See below) Letting my imagina-
tion run wild, I see the bishop, after Princeton, going to
Rome. There, the Pope, following an ancient custom when eminent confessors came to call on the Successor of Peter,
whose duty it is "to confirm his brethren in their faith"
(Luke 22:32), goes out to the City's limits and meets his
guest at Fumicino Airport. Rumor has it that Bishop Kong
is the Cardinal-designate in petto. So the Pope has a surprise for him: then and there he confers on Kong the sacred
pallium. The ceremony is on TV, and beamed to China...

Back to reality! Bishop Ting gave many press conferences.
On September 9, he preached at Riverside Church, New York,
on "man, i.e., ourselves." From September 8 to 26, at the
invitation of the National Council of Churches, the group
stayed in the U.S.A., travelling extensively and meeting
with all kinds of people. Ms. Jean Woo, the wife of Franklin Woo, editor of China Notes, accompanied the group on
their American trip. She wrote a 7-page account, entitled
"Generating Human Warmth and Friendship."

In Chicago, at the end of September, the Chinese visitors
were guests at events sponsored by the University of Chicago
Divinity School, the Lutheran School of Theology at Chicago,
and the Catholic Theological Union. Robert Schreiter, co-
director with this author of The Chicago Institute of Theology and Culture, organized, in collaboration with others,
a colloquium on "Theological Education Today in the U.S.
and China." His report, especially written for this volume,
is found below, Chapter 6.

Dr Ting told a Chicago Sun-Times reporter that westerners
must realize three things:

-- that the Chinese, religious and otherwise, have no desire
   to import western personnel and money.

-- that the churches in China are, and probably will continue to be, less institutionalized, less clericalized and
   more lay-oriented than western churches.

-- that the Chinese interest in "house churches" does not
   mean the churches are part of an underground movement.
   "Now that more church buildings are being reopened and
   renovated, there is likely to be a growing interest in
   public religious services." But Bishop Ting also pre-
   dicted that the meetings in homes will be continuing
   as a healthy feature of Chinese religious life.

Roy Larson, the reporter, then asked him this question:

"What distinctive gift China's 700,000 Protestants and
3-million Catholics have to offer the worldwide ecumenical church?" To which Bishop Ting gave this answer:
"The church in China is the first one in the world that
has existed in a post-colonial, post-feudalistic socialist society. In a sense, the church in our country is
a laboratory where experiments are being carried out
that will be of benefit to the church in the whole world."
(September 22, 1979)

From the U.S., K.H. Ting went to Canada where he visited
for six weeks in October and November. For him it was a
reunion, as he had lived in Toronto in the late 1940's working with the SCM. His Canadian visit was in response to
a joint invitation of the University of Toronto, York University, and the Canada China Program of the Canadian Council of Churches. His many conferences and radio talks are
about to appear in print.

As I have done in the case of Mr Zhao Fusan, I should now
like to quote a number of statements which help us understand Bishop Ting's position on Protestant Christianity in
China. As in previous cases, I start with his address to
the Japanese Buddhist group which visited China in April
1974, to whom he was introduced as "The representative of
the All China Three-Self Movement." These were his words:

We rejoice in the visit of the Niwano group to China.
As in China all religions are equal, Protestants only
amount to 1/1000th of the population. They are not
subject to any social discrimination and their rights
and duties are the same of all other people.

Communist Party members are atheists, and spread their
ideas. These ideas are not forced upon people. Revolution and reconstruction are the common goals of all.
The Communist Party is bringing all people together in
the reconstruction of the country, and as religious
people also collaborate in this effort, the result is
truly remarkable.

Protestantism has come to China about 100 years ago
from the West. Missionaries have come but we have
read that they were the forerunners of an invasion
of our people and of our land. Imperialism by force
of battleships and canon imposed upon China the Unequal
Treaties. On the strength of these Treaties, missionaries could penetrate deeply into the Chinese hinterland.

As a matter of fact, these missionaries who were working
in far away places sent all sorts of information to the
imperialists. There were missionaries who, in connivance

with landowners and bandits, became extorsionists to
the Chinese people.

Many missionaries managed hospitals and schools in
China. They bought the Chinese people at the price
of a little gooddoing and thereby they became accom-
lices of the imperialist penetration of China. There
is a saying by one of the British governors of South
Africa: "To take the liberty of the natives away, one
missionary can do the same job as one regiment." These
words are also applicable to China. Whenever one Protestant is born in China, the Chinese nation loses one
citizen. This is sad, but it is a fact. Hence, Protestants in this country rejoice in their liberation
and if, under the leadership of the Communist Party,
Christians would walk the socialist road, this would
truly be a blessing.

Protestants in this country also oppose imperialism
and endorse socialism. I myself have been educated in
the West, and in the past I felt prejudices against
Communism. At one time I was entrusted with work in
an international organization. When I prepared to return to China, my associates told me: "When you return
they shall cut your throat or send you to a concentration camp."

Facts were quite different. My head is still upon my
shoulders. I have never been in a concentration camp
and I continue to work as a Christian. I support the
policy of self-government, self-sufficiency and self-
propagation which are the characteristics of an indep-
endent church. As there are no longer foreign missionaries and as we do no longer receive financial support
from abroad, we are no longer under foreign orders.

We should like to change the former attitude of Protestantism. We should like the Church to remain pure.
We intend to continue courageously so as not to frus-
trate the hope that is in us.

It must not be forgotten that the above words were pronounced when the evil Gang of Four were at the height of
their power. Twenty years earlier, friends remember, Dr
Ting displayed remarkable courage. On June 12, 1957, he
delivered a much-acclaimed address to the students of Nanjing Theological Seminary whose president he then was. His
theme: "Christian Theism." The speech was Ting's unblinking
challenge to Communist materialism.

A few months ago, Peter Lee recalled this speech.(Jones:
156-67) He was moved to write:

It was a quiet but authentic affirmation of faith made against the atheistic background of Communism. While he thought that certain positive things could be said about Communism, he remained unwaveringly a theist. He did not think that the new China has taken care of the sinful nature of man just because it has brought about a more just social environment. He appealed to his listeners to turn to Jesus Christ for the forgiveness of sin... On reading Ting's address on theism and his other writings, one would be grossly unfair if one should call him a betrayer of Jesus Christ. (CF, 2:68)

I do not know Bishop Ting, and it is not for me to judge his person, his intentions, or the orthodoxy of his faith. To help the reader better to understand his thought, here are sixteen key statements which he recently made:

-- On the Gang of Four: "With the downfall of the Gang of Four we are coming out of a period during which there were many violations of religious rights, and the policy of religious freedom is beginning to be put into practice again... During the Cultural Revolution, the situation was quite different. In those years, the influence of the Gang of Four gained the upper hand, and it was a great disadvantage to religious believers. I know of Muslims, for instance, who were compelled to raise pigs, and they were even compelled to eat pork. When they refused, the bones of hogs were poured into the wells so that the Muslims would find it impossible to drink the water of the wells." (C&C, 9-12:1-2)

-- On the Cultural Revolution: "The Cultural Revolution was directly responsible for the de-institutionalization of Protestant Christianity in China and for the emergence for the first time in Chinese history of a Christianity fully integrated into Chinese life. In this sense this ten year period was formative for the Chinese church. At the same time it has not been easy with the enforced isolation of Christians from each other, the destruction of Bibles and other books, and in a few places, such as Shanghai, the suppression of all forms of Christian life which in these places could only continue in secret.

It would, however, be wrong to think that this was the case generally. In Nanjing, for example, after the initial Red Guard onslaught, Christians were able to meet quietly, but openly, during all these years. The process of structural dissolution during this period caused problems for some Christians, especially for those related in the past to the more liturgically centred churches.

In particular, many of the clergy found the adjustment
hard since they found themselves laicized and compelled
to take secular jobs. Yet, on the whole, the experience
has been a positive one, and one which many would not
wish to abandon in favor of a return to more formal
structures. At the present time, with the re-emergence
of public worship in church buildings and of some full-
time clergy there is disagreement on a number of questions."(IL, 12:13-4)

-- On the Three-Self Movement: "There is no objection to
international connections between Chinese Christians
and Christians abroad, but it is just that the churches
must be self-supporting, self-governing, and the work of
the churches is to be carried on by Chinese Christians
themselves. That is the Three-Self Movement.

In theological education for instance, we felt that it
was necessary for education to be carried on in Chinese,
not always lecturing in the English language. We don't
want to make theological students less Chinese after
five years of education. So I don't think the churches
in China would welcome western missionaries. But we are
not really against missionaries as individuals, because
many of them came to China with the sole intention of
evangelising China.

They did not want to be a political tool of western penetration, but they were caught in a whole machinery of
western military and political penetration of China...
It is unthinkable for the Chinese churches to receive
missionaries back as permanent co-workers."(C&C, 9-12:2)

-- On the role of religion: "As with other Christians we
contacted in China, both Ting and Chao asked the same
essential questions. 'What is the social role and significance of religion in today's unjust world?' Ting said
that what has been happening in China since the revolution had implications far beyond the borders of the PRC.
The need to find the social role and significance of
religion has been demonstrated by China, which according
to Ting is an 'object lesson' for all Christians everywhere."(Jean & Franklin Woo, in CN, 16/4-17/1:53)

-- On the amendment of the Constitution: "Bishop Ting spoke
of the proposal by religious leaders who form the delegation to the CPPCC to the National People's Congress
that the wording of the Constitution be changed. The
1978 Constitution retains the wording of the 1975 Constitution concerning "Freedom to believe in religion, not
to believe in religion and the freedom to propagate
atheism."

It is proposed that this should revert to the original
1954 wording: "Freedom to believe in religion." According to Ting, the present wording is the result of
ultra-left influence and is unbalanced, providing constitutional excuse for future leftist excesses. The
NPC is now looking into the matter and it is likely that
the wording will be changed at its next meeting."(Bob
Whyte, in IL, 12:20)

-- On patriotism: "In the face of repressive attitudes
toward religion, especially during the period of the
'ultra-leftist' Gang of Four, all Chinese Christians
had to confront the question of whether to be patriotic
or unpatriotic. According to the bishop, patriotism
'has a different meaning in China; it has to do with
conservation. In China patriotism means for Christians
to identify ourselves with the cause of our people's
liberation' -- which he and the other delegation members did." (Linda Marie Delloff, The Christian Century,
October 24)

-- On Christians as Chinese: "Bearing what we get out of
the New Testament in mind, we listen to the Chinese revolutionaries who point out how our people have suffered
under and are still bearing the consequences of the oppression of imperialism, bureaucratic capitalism and
feudalism, commonly called the three mountains.

There is an area where Christians and the rest of the
Chinese have come to see eye to eye. This common ground,
with common language, as we say, is important to us because, standing upon this common ground, the evangelist
can speak as one among the people and not as one speaking
from abroad or from above or from outside. He speaks
out of true love for the people and is free from the mis-
anthropic Jonah mentality, with all its abhorrence of
the people to whom he is sent." (Riverside Church sermon,
IL, 10:19)

-- On house-churches: "Now that liberalized policies will
allow the congregations to return to their institutional
facilities, Bishop Ting is not sure that all groups will
do so. People enjoy the personal contact and intimate
atmosphere of the small in-home gatherings. One area of
concern right now is whether a shift back to institutional settings would necessitate increasing the numbers
of ordained clergy -- a change from the mutual, nonor-
dained ministering that goes on in the small informal
meetings. Many groups simply do not want an ordained
minister, and wish to remain self-governing and self-
propagating."(The Christian Century, October 24)

-- On evangelism: "There is no objection to evangelism as such, because freedom of religion does involve the freedom to tell others of our religious faith. This happened even during the days of the Gang of Four." (C&C, 9-12:3)

-- On church unity: "It is hoped that none of the present disagreements need prevent some sort of united church structure from emerging in the next year, but any such structure would need to be very simple and would not seek to impose any conformity on the diversity of Christian life in China. Thus a national structure should neither detract from the vitality of the house-churches which have been a real source of renewal for Christian life nor seek to detract from the natural leadership that has emerged over the past fifteen years." (IL, 12:15)

-- On church growth in China: "Christianity is growing in China, contends Bishop Ting, and it is also reaching out for conversation with other faiths. Although there is at present no organized ecumenical movement in the country, representatives of different religions -- and spokespersons for various views within the Christian spectrum -- are now in closer contact with each other." (The Christian Century, October 24)

-- On Protestant overseas Chinese: "Could Protestant overseas Chinese come to China and be involved in the church?" "I have never heard any proposition of that sort so far. But theoretically there should be no problem, because they are Chinese. Practically, however, there are probably many problems. These Chinese have lived abroad, and they will have to face new problems when they settle down in China, when they try to really identify with the ordinary people in China. Before they can really do that, I wonder if they could be of very great help to the Chinese Christian groups." (C&C, 9-12:3)

-- On relations with the World Council of Churches: "Church leaders haven't discussed the World Council of Churches for many years. What posture is to be assumed with regard to WCC membership will be a forthcoming topic for the 150-member National Committee of Churches when it meets... The Committee has not met during the years of the Cultural Revolution and is now in process of restoring its functions." (WCC, Ecum. Press Service, 9/13)

-- On Catholics in China: "The formation of a national non-Roman Catholic church body, interrupted by the Cultural Revolution, to represent 'post-denominational Christianity' in China has now been taken up again. There are about 3 million Roman Catholics and 700,000 Protestants in the country." (Ibid.)

-- On theological training: "The lack of a theologically trained leadership has led to the growth of a number of undesirable phenomena. A relatively common problem has been the growth of doctrinal aberrations and this problem has been exacerbated by the lack of Bibles and of people trained in the exposition of scriptures. One result of this has been the stress in some places on 'personal testimonies' leading all too frequently to increasingly unorthodox tendencies and to a loss of direction." (Bob Whyte, in IL, 12:14)

-- On theological reconstruction: "Biship Ting feels that Christians in China have, as a result of their experience under socialism, come to understand that God is active through the revolution and in the lives of non-believers as well as through the Church. This has meant a profound shift in theological perspective. At the same time, religious experience is distinct from political experience and for this reason Chinese Christians have reservations about the "theology of liberation," although they approve of its identification with the poor and oppressed. (Ibid.)

-- On Jesuit priests being asked to return to China: "As far as I know, the attitude of the government towards the Jesuits would be that it is a private matter for one to be a Jesuit. If he is very good in some specialization, and if he is qualified in other ways, then he might be invited. I know of a Roman Catholic nun who is a teacher in Beijing University. The fact that she is a nun is a private matter. In China, religion is regarded as a private matter. So there is no law that forbids a Jesuit from being a teacher in a Chinese university. I noticed that there was some talk about Jesuits having been invited by Chinese authorities to return to China and open a Jesuit institution. Have you heard of that? Well, that is not true, because I am sure that China is not going to restore any missionary or Jesuit university. (C&C, 9-12:12)

Let us now return to Bishop Ting and his fellow-delegates at Princeton. The WCRP III report or "Princeton Declaration" is a 46-page, well-illustrated pamphlet that sums up the findings of the Conference and gives a list of the participants. The Declaration has a fairly long paragraph, entitled "Religion in Socialist Societies," which is specially interesting within the framework of Bishop Ting's ideas.

First, there is reference to Buddhists and Muslims in the U.S.S.R.:

They are given the same status as other religious followers. The non-religious also receive equality of

treatment. There is no conflict among the groups. The
religious group does not impose its will upon the government in governmental matters, and the government
does not impose its will upon religious groups in religious matters. The Buddhists have actively participated
in iternational forums for peace. They are most desir-
ous of developing close contacts with the Chinese Buddhists.

Then follows a statement describing religious conditions
in the PRC. Althoughmuch of it has a familiar ring, I shall
quote it in full:

The Chinese participants explained that, although before
liberation in 1949, there were many instances of non-
cooperation among different religious traditions, inter-
religious relations have undergone significant changes
since the establishment of the People's Republic. Representatives of different traditions have come together
often to discuss important matters of common concern, to
learn from each other how better to serve the people,
and to devote themselves to the cause of socialist construction. Religious freedom, national equality, and
the practice of the social customs of the various nationalities are ensured by law.

Article 46 of the Constitution explicitly stipulates
that all citizens are free to believe in religion, free
not to believe in religion, and free to propagate atheism. (The Gang of Four and other ultra-Leftists used
this clause over the last decade or so to claim that
religion cannot be propagated, but 16 religious leaders
from various traditions in the Chinese People's Political Committee Conference recently proposed to the National People's Congress that this constitutional phrase
be changed to read simply that "all Chinese citizens
are free to believe in religion," so that such claims
could never be made again in the future).

The newly-adopted Penal Code of China in Article 147
provides a penalty of two years' imprisonment for sub-
stantial interference by any government officer with
the people's rights to religious freedom. Although
the Gang of Four brought about serious damage to religious freedom and equality, today in China there is no
religious discrimination, and people are free to enjoy
a normal religious life and participate in religious
activities. Steps are being taken to rectify the errors and redress the wrongs of the Gang of Four.

Although people of different religious traditions have
worked together in China, they have not worshipped

together in the last 30 years, and Chinese delegates to
WCRP III have observed with interest the multi-religious
worship at St. Patrick's Cathedral and the daily morning
services at Princeton. They have asked for further enlightenment regarding multi-religious services, since
they are still not convinced of their value.

As an old-timer at WCRP Conferences I know that it is
de rigueur, in the final declaration, to accommodate the
national delegations. One Seminar group brought up conflict
areas by name: Albania, Canada, East Timor, Ethiopia, Europe, India, Iran, Japan, Korea, Latin America, the Middle
East, the Netherlands, Northern Ireland, Philippines, South-
east Asia, Southern Africa, Turkey, and West Iran. China
was not included.

As an invitee of the National Council of Churches, Bishop
Ting was confronted with a difficult situation immediately
upon his arrival at New York. The Dalai Lama too had been
invited by the Church World Service of NCC the day before
the visit of the Christian delegates from China.

K.H. Ting was briefed on the situation upon his arrival
at the airport. His first reaction was not negative; but
on the following day NCC was informed that the situation
could not be accepted because the simultaneous invitiation
of the Dalai Lama might be interpreted as an interference
in the internal affairs of China. Ting suggested that NCC
should make it clear that 1) the invitation to the Dalai
Lama was not endorsed by NCC as such; 2) that the Dalai
Lama should not speak to the press during his visit there,
as the Chinese delegation would otherwise be obliged to
make a public statement also; 3) that NCC should state that
Tibet was an integral part of China. I do not know the
final outcome of this incident, apart from the fact that an
emergency meeting was held and a NCC delegation decided to
go to Princeton and talk directly to the Chinese delegates.

+
+   +
+

How long will the present religious situation last? Will
it improve, or deteriorate? Will influential people such as
Zhao Fusan and K.H. Ting be given strength to guide it in
the right direction? These are weighty questions to which I
find no answer.

Father Lazslo Ladany, S.J., one of the oldest and best-informed watchers of the China scene, and since 1953 editor of the forthnightly China News Analysis, at his own risk, made this prediction in a June interview:

> Religious freedom is slowly returning in China but the Catholics and Protestants who suffered most for their beliefs in the past are not enthusiastic. They foresee that the government will allow some religious activity but will organize and control this through the same Christian leaders who they feel compromised the faith previously by collaborating with the government.
>
> The Communists proceeded cautiously. Using sympathizers among the religious leaders, they sought to split the ranks of the believers, establishing a communist-ruled national association for each religion and imposing sentences of imprisonment or hard labor on those who resisted. Many died in prisons and camps. Nevertheless an appearance of freedom of religion was maintained until the Cultural Revolution, with religious services in a few, well-controlled temples and churches. When the Cultural Revolution broke out, the red guards were ordered to sweep away all traces of "superstition," and churches and temples and even private homes were invaded and ransacked.
>
> Many observers were surprised by the courage of the Chinese Christians. Of all the religious groups, the Catholics put up the strongest resistance. The majority of bishops, priests and laity refused to cooperate with the government's plans, especially its attempts to have them disown any links with Rome. They did far better than the English bishops and people in the time of Henry VIII. We don't know what the resisters will do now. Probably they won't go to church unless they are forced.

Ladany then rang a warning bell for those of us who think they know what is going on in China:

> Far away someone may think he understands China, but the observer up close knows clearly that he doesn't understand that huge, complex and ancient land. The strength of China is the culture, industry and resiliency of its people. These undergird and outlast all the regimes and their policies. (IHD, 6:16-9)

While we prayerfully await the outcome of the tragic confrontation between China and the Church, the moment has come for a vibrant salute to one of the greatest peoples on earth. Wan-sui, wan-sui to the Chinese people!

Chapter 6:

Bishop Ting at a theological conference in Chicago

The four Christian leaders who visited Chicago September
19-20, 1979, were all part of the Three Self Movement. One
of the prime considerations here was a discussion of theological
education and research, since Chicago is one of the major centers
for both of these in the United States.

A discussion of where theological education and research
might be going in China today gives some glimpse of the situation
at least among Protestants. To this end, a colloquium on
"Theological Education Today in the U.S. and China" was organized
by me in cooperation with the Chicago Cluster of Theological
Schools and the Divinity School of the University of Chicago.
It was held at the Divinity School on September 20.

There were participants from eight of the theological
schools in the Chicago area: Bethany Theological Seminary,
Catholic Theological Union, Jesuit School of Theology, Lutheran
School of Theology, McCormick Theological Seminary, Meadville/
Lombard Theological School, and Northern Baptist Theological
Seminary, and the Divinity School of the University of Chicago.

There were two purposes for the colloquium. First of all,
the colloquium was intended to inform the Chinese of directions
which theological education and research had taken in the
thirty years since the liberation. They had requested such a
meeting to give them an update on what had been happening here.
Particularly in the years of the Cultural Revolution there had
been no contact with theological circles outside China. To
this end, representatives from the theological schools presented
various aspects of theological education and research: the
new ecumenical relationships, the role of women, non-seminary
based education programs, the phenomenon of clustering, developments in continuing education for clergy, new directions in
systematic theology, the growth of clinical and field education,
the shift into the social sciences as an ancillary discipline
for theology.

The second purpose was to give the Chinese an opportunity to respond to U.S. developments, and share with the educators gathered the directions of theological education and research in China. Two veteran theological educators, K. H. Ting and Chen Chi-ming, Principal and Dean of the former Nanking Theological College respectively, spoke for the situation in China.

Bishop Ting outlined some of the significant changes which have followed the downfall of the Gang of Four. The reopening of many Churches (notably the large Moore Memorial Church in Shanghai had just opened prior to the colloquium; a thousand people had attended the first service there), and the discussions surrounding article 46 in the Constitution regarding religious freedom were perhaps the most notable shifts. These changes provide a climate in which other developments might take place.

Within that framework, the amalgamation of the Nanking Theological Seminary into Nanking University as its Center for Religious Studies is also a significant event. The Center will serve primarily as a research institute for the advanced study of Christianity.(The Institute for the Study of World Religions in Peking will study other major religious traditions) The program would be a two-year graduate sequence for advanced university students. In addition, the Center would provide courses in the history of religious thought for the philosophy and history departments of the University, as well as engage in some interdisciplinary work with the departments. And finally, the Center would be responsible for translating major works of religious thought into Chinese. It is currently preparing and overseeing a new translation of the Bible.

In its teaching and research, the primary methodological approaches at the Center will be historical and sociological. This would indicate that the Center sees as its primary constituency the university rather than the churches. Mr Chen showed a keen interest in developments in the sociology of religion and indicated that it would be a major discipline at the Center. The study of religion at the Center will thus not reflect a confessional stance as much as its role in the building of society and its place as part of a total mosaic in the history of culture.

But what will become of theological education as such? Prior to the liberation, Nanking Theological Seminary had served as a united seminary for the training of conciliar Protestants and many Evangelical Christians. Bishop Ting indicated that there would be a need for a different kind of theological education for ministry in China today. The ecclesiological picture has changed. Rather than pastors serving large or far-flung parishes, the past thirty years has seen the emergence and growth of what the West would

call the house church. Religious activity has centered upon
the family, the home, the small group. While this may have
served as a way of protecting one's religious commitment in
times of persecution in the past, its primary focus is that
this is a more Chinese way to worship. It reflects the fact
that religion for the laity in China has traditionally been
a decentralized, non-institutionalized reality placed within
the context of a family. As a result, a generation of Christian
are growing up who have experienced Christianity without the
mediation of professionally trained clergy. With the possibility of developing programs for training clergy at this time,
what will most likely happen is that these Christians are not
interested in having them.

The kind of church order which grows out of this will have
a distinctively Chinese character. Western church leaders may
be a bit uneasy with this development; how, for example, can
faithful interpretations of the Scriptures and church traditions
be assured in this kind of environment? What happens to a
sacramental structure? But Westerners are also faced here
with something else. For a number of years now, theologians
and church leaders have been calling for a contextualization
of theology and church life, which goes beyond mere adaptation
to assuming the thought and life patterns of a culture. This
seems to be going on in one way in China today. Will we have
the courage to live up to our words in this instance? Church
experiments need to mature over time. Yet we have a living
experience of Christianity here that seems to continue without
some of the forms of clerical mediation which has been part
of the Western Christian experience for centuries. It deserves
time to grow and develop.

Some Westerners may feel that the relation of these
decentralized Church groupings to the national structure (in
this case, the Three Self Movement) might produce a nationalist
rather than a national church, with the consequence of a
Christianity in subservience to the State. Again, one should
not be hasty in drawing this conclusion. Even in the Western
Christian experience, a variety of relationships have been
taken with the State. These grow out of much more complex
histories than simple surrender of the Gospel. One thinks,
for example, of Orthodoxy, where close relations with the State
is part of the sacramentalization of the cosmos. One needs
to look at the local churches, the Three Self Movement, and
the People's Republic in light of Chinese history rather than
Western history. It will be in that context that judgments
might be able to be made at some point in the future.

An important notion stressed by Ting and others has been
that developments in China are an attempt to be genuinely
Christian and genuinely Chinese at the same time. We need
to watch what is happening in China through Chinese eyes, rather
than Western ones.

In its attempt to be truely Christian and truely Chinese, however, there is one caveat which fellow Christians can justifiably raise; namely, a Church which closes in on itself entirely runs the risk of ceasing to be the Church of Christ. Catholicity and outreach, as well as mutual correction, are signs of the presence of the living Gospel. In reaction to imperialist moves from other countries, and from some misguided missionary movements, the Church in China is drawing back and trying to insure itself against the mistakes of the past. This would seem to be a justified response. But how will the opening into the ecumenical Church be achieved?

Western Christians must allow the Chinese themselves to make these first determinations. And there are some indications already present which give a partial vision of how that future might be realized. The Center for Religious Studies is not only open to, but hungry for, recent Western religious scholarship. They have accepted offers of books to rebuild the library. Orbis Books offered both the Peking and the Nanking centers a selection of their publications; the Catholic Theological Union has offered the Nanking Center a library of some sixty-five hundred volumes, both monographs and periodicals. Secondly, they are open to visiting lecturers at some point in the reasonably near future. At the present time, the new Center is still being organized; but they expressed the hope of inviting scholars in Christian thought sometime fairly soon. Thus, the Chinese are open to recent Western thought; one would hope that this kind of channel would allow for communication, yet allow Chinese to assimilate recent developments in a distinctively Chinese fashion.

Questions of course will need to be raised about how leadership for the future will be trained. But perhaps it is still too early to press that question. Nonetheless, it will need to be raised as Chinese Christians take their place once again among their brothers and sisters in World Christianity.

The discussion here does not take into account the situation of Catholic Christians in China. The four Chinese visitors, all members of the Three Self Movement, did not seem to have had much contact with members of the Patriotic Association or with other Catholics. Because of the structure of Catholic church polity, the problems here are of a different nature than they are for Protestants. But to say much about them here would be too speculative to be really helpful in the current situation. One would hope that regularized contacts with Chinese Catholics in the Patriotic Association could be established soon.

Robert Schreiter
Catholic Theological Union
The Chicago Institute of Theology and Culture

November 23, 1979

Chapter 7:

Bishop Moser visits the PRC

The outstanding Catholic visitor of the year to China is Dr Georg Moser, bishop of Rottenburg-Stuttgart and leader of the Pax Christi movement in Germany.

The bishop visited China from November 1 to 12, accompanied by Prälat Eberhard Mühlbacher, as member of an official delegation of Baden-Württemberg under the leadership of Minister-president Lothar Späth. Another member of this distinguished group was Professor Klaus Mehnert, author of the well-known book China nach dem Sturm, Stuttgart: Deutsche Verlags-Anstalt, 1971.

The German press has given considerable attention to Bishop Moser's trip because he was the first bishop to meet with Premier Hua Guofeng and with the newly nominated bishop of Beijing, Fu Tieshan. Hence the somewhat lengthy account which follows. My sources are dispatches of the Katholische Nachrichten Agentur (KNA), November 14-5, an article in the Frankfurter Allgemeine Zeitung, dated Beijing, November 11 and published the following day, an account of the trip by Prälat Mühlbacher in the Würzburger Kath. Sonntagsblatt, December 2, as well as information from private sources. Quotations below are the words of Bishop Moser, unless otherwise marked. First, the KNA interview with him:

-- What does your visit mean to the Chinese Catholics?

-- "A most difficult question. Our information about Chinese Catholics is hazy because we only were allowed to have contact with representatives of the so-called Patriotic Church which is the officially recognized Catholic organization. We could not meet with other Catholics or their spokespersons. I hope there will be no disappointment on this fact. We did everything we could, but it was in vain. Nevertheless, I do not want to sound negative. In general, our conversations with four representatives of the Patriotic Church took

place in a very friendly and open atmosphere, and we
discussed some critical matters as well."

-- Also about the situation in which Catholics loyal to
Rome find themselves?

-- "Of course we talked about it, and also about other deli-
cate questions. That we succeeded for the first time in
making contact, this in itself, I feel, is very important.
Here a Chinese proverb is appropriate: "Beter to see once
than to hear a hundred times."

-- Did you also have the impression, in your conversations
with political leaders, that "something is moving" as
Pope John-Paul II has said about the relations of the
Catholic Church with China?

-- "In general, yes."

-- Can we sum up and say: it was a beginning?

-- "My trip could perhaps be a beginning of a dialogue which
would very carefully explore the background and the bur-
ning problems which we face. In our conversations there
were open questions and there were also difficult questions. There are barriers which we must take very seriously. But there are also first indications of really
good opportunities for dialogue and of a certain willingness to continue the dialogue on the level which we have
been able to reach."

Bishop Moser inquired also about Protestants in China. He
stressed the importance of an ecumenical approach of the
churches in their relations with China. "The divisions
among Christians obscure the Gospel in Chinese eyes. Conse-
quently, the Good News fails to become a saving alternative
to the danger of pure positivism and secularization to which
China is exposed."

Bishop Moser countered the widely accepted opinion that
the Chinese are pragmatists rather than searchers for God,
and that they are fascinated by technical progress and have
little attention left for matters of the spirit. "People,
also in China," the bishop said, "are incurably religious."

Christianity in China refused to die during the last
very difficult thirty years. Particularly Chinese youth
ask questions about Christianity. Christian life continues in the house churches. Contact with the world
Church and with the Pope has not been severed. A great
number of Christians listen to Radio Veritas broadcasts

from Manila. Many more people in China than we think
are waiting for more than scientific progress. The
Church should take this into account, and try to meet
them.

Minister-president Späth showed considerable courage in
having Bishop Moser accompany his group, and in this he
went against the advice of the German Embassy in Beijing.
The embassy's worries proved perfectly groundless. The
bishop was received with unfailing courtesy. Premier Hua
(whom he had met at a Stuttgart reception during the
Premier's recent trip to Germany) did not utter a word of
criticism or of surprise about the bishop's presence; nor
did the Foreign Ministry. Pope John-Paul II knew about
the event, but sent no instructions. As far as I know,
the only word to come from Rome was a private letter from
a Chinese priest suggesting some questions which the bishop
might want to ask. In fact, Bishop Moser needed no coach-
ing and no credentials: he is the Pax Christi president of
Germany, and as such he has travelled widely on prickly
missions for peace.

The bishop was told that the Vatican's relations with
the PRC are poisoned by the former's relations with Taiwan. On this matter, the bishop feels, time will be the
healer. A visit of the Pope to Beijing, he thought, "is
not realistic." He would prefer other contacts at the episcopal level.

As he told us already, the bishop deplored that he was
not allowed to have contact with "Catholics loyal to Rome,
with the grassroots Church." The very mentioning of that
Church was taboo to his partners in dialogue. The bishop,
throughout his trip, remained aware of the fact that he
might give the impression to the Catholics whom he could
not meet that people in high places, such as himself, were
trying to arrange matters over their heads, a fact which
he publicly deplored and for which he apologized.

The German visitors felt that the government had started with the rehabilitation of some Catholics, but that
they took back with one hand what they gave with the other.
Those Catholics who had been condemned for crimes against
the law or the state received no amnesty. The bishop was
informed that "many Catholics refuse the guidance of the
government." He felt that an outsider like himself stood
no chance of being told by people in authority about the
criteria which determine someone's release from prison.

For Moser and Mühlbacher it became evident that "the most
crucial point of our conversation was the opposition
between the Patriotic and the Roman Catholics." Yet the
bishop deprecates the use of the word "schism" in relation

to the Patriotics who, he feels, are "Catholics living in
an emergency situation for which there are no ready-made
categories which apply."

Bishop Moser thinks that there are more bridges to the
Catholic Patriotic Church than we think. The world Church
should soberly assess the social and historical background
from which the Patriotic Church arose, and in which its
members live. With great care and realism, we should try
to improve the overall situation of all Catholics in China.
The newly appointed Bishop Fu Tieshan told Bishop Moser:
"When all is said and done, we are not strangers but brethren in the faith." And, the bishop feels, this applies to
the members of the Patriotic Church as well: "They show no
anti-Roman feelings."

Whether Catholicism will survive in China depends on the
quality and number of priests available as pastors and
bishops. All priests from the Mao era are older than fifty
and no new priests have been ordained since 1955. At present, the formation of priests is never mentioned; nor could
it take place.

The community of priests at Beijing's Nan-tang, which is
often in the news, is not normative for other priests in
the country. The fourteen priests in that community belong
to the Patriotic Church which follows the "illegitimately
consecrated bishops" of the fifties. According to convergent testimonies of other Catholics, some 80% of all Cath-
clic priests remained "loyal to Rome." For this they were
severely punished.

Yet it is a fact that, at present, no priests are in prison because their long terms of 20, 25 and 30 years have now
expired. Church-and-China watchers divide priests under
four categories:

-- Priests, like those at the Nantang who can say Mass,
   hear confessions and receive visitors.

-- Priests who were in prison or under house-arrest and had
   their civil rights restored. Such priests have a place
   for work and receive a salary of 30 yuan (2 yuan is somewhat more than 1 US-dollar). These priests live in private homes and enjoy freedom of movement. Taking appropriate precautions, they occasionally administer the
   sacraments. I heard a few days ago that one priest was
   arrested for hearing someone's confession.

-- Old priests and those uncapable of work. They stay with
   relatives who must support them as they cannot live on
   the 16 yuan allowance which they receive.

-- Priests who do not enjoy full freedom of movement, and
who live in communities to which the authorities assign
a type of forced labor. Thus there is a group of twenty
priests living at Ya-er street, No. 50, near the Kuolo
Gate in Beijing, who make boxes for pharmaceutical products. They refuse all visitors.

There is a similar group living in Changchun. It consists of Catholic priests and Buddhist monks. In Shanghai, there is a community of thirty priests, ten of whom
are Jesuits, and of twenty sisters, who weave mats.
Close to a Buddhist temple in Wuhan, there is another
"ecumenical" community of priests and bonzes who work
for the government. Finally, recent Hong Kong reports
mention a community of seven priests in Kaifeng.(KNA)

Bishop Moser was strongly grieved at being refused permission to visit Ignatius Kong Pingmei, the Jesuit bishop
of Shanghai who was arrested in September 1955 and sentenced
to twenty years or life, a sentence which was communicated
to the press only on March 17, 1960. Kong had been tried
for treason, the government announced, and found guilty. At
that time, he was 69. Only in 1977 did we hear that the
bishop is still alive. Moser's request was curtly turned
down with the words that "Bishop Kong remains obstinate in
his loyalty to Rome; he committed a grievous offense against
the state." Now, it must be admitted that Bishop Kong was
the strongest opponent of the Patriotic Church. However,
other reports have it that Bishop Kong was offered his freedom but that he refused to accept it until all other Catholic prisoners would be freed. Bishop Moser also failed
to meet another Jesuit bishop, Dominic Tang of Canton, already in prison for more than a quarter-century...

Upon his arrival in Beijing, Bishop Moser had requested
to be allowed to say Mass at the Nan-tang, the Cathedral
of the Immaculate Conception. It is well-known that this
is the only church open in Beijing at which Mass is celebrated on Sundays, especially for the benefit of foreign
diplomats and visitors. The bishop was left in uncertainty until the last moment when a car showed up at his hotel
to bring him to church. He donned his episcopal robes and
pectoral cross. At the entrance of the Cathedral, Moser
was solemnly welcomed by a priest who knelt and kissed his
ring. He was then ushered into the front bench. At that
very moment, a Chinese priest started Mass, in Latin and
back turned toward the congregation. The bishop thus lost
the opportunity to say Mass and, as he had wished to do,
give his blessing.

Bishop Moser also learned that 20 to 25 canonically consecrated bishops live as simple citizens and without

exercising any episcopal functions. There is no communication among bishops; the one does no longer know of the existence of the other.

Patriotic bishops, such as Chang Qiashu of Shanghai, whom Bishop Moser met, play a political rather than a religious role. Police told Moser that Monsignor Paul Chang Shenkuo, Apostolic Administrator of Sipingkai in Manchuria, was released from prison and is now living in the mining town of Huinan, 300 kilometers of Changshun, where he works.

Bishop Matthew Tuan Inmin, of Wanxian, works for the local Revolutionary Committee, i.e., for the city. Matthew Wang Weimin, uncanonically consecrated bishop of Kirin, is married, has no children, and lives in Changshun. He too makes medecine boxes. Another illegitimate bishop, Wang Ruijia, of Harbin, lives like an ordinary citizen at home.

During the last months of the year, many priests have been seen in public again. My own confrere, Father Joseph Chang, 75, from whom there was no news since 1955, recently sent word that he is in good health and has not forgotten the religious family to which he belongs. (I for one marvel at the extraordinary stamina of so many Chinese priests and bishops who spent years in circumstances which would have killed much younger men. I know from personal experience what concentration camps are!)

Legitimate or illegitimate, Catholics, priests and bishops, suffered without distinction during the Cultural Revolution. Their scars, physical and psychological remain.

Bishop Moser, like all other visitors, was constantly reminded of the evil Gang of Four. Under the Gang, arrests were arbitrary. Many Catholics were sent to jail without being accused of any specific crime. Some were released in 1973, also without being told the reason.

He who serves a prison term vanishes completely from sight. Generally, there are no visits, no correspondence. All prisoners are expected to make a self-indictment, because all are presumed guilty. Eventually, the prisoner may come to trial, without a defense lawyer and in sessions closed to the public. Until recently, Article 10 of a 1951 law was often invoked to justify imprisonment: "Anyone who attempts to sow discord between the various national minorities, the democratic classes, the various democratic and popular groups, or who attempts to weaken the bonds that unite the population with the government... as well as anyone who engages in counterrevolutionary propaganda, or invents or repeats false rumors, upon conviction, will receive a minimum of three years in prison and a maximum of death."

Until the end of the fifties, some laws were written down. During the Cultural Revolution the profession of lawyer was abolished. The Gang of Four, in what is now called "a streak of mysticism," insisted that the people of China were politically so well educated that they were capable of defending, accusing, and condemning themselves without the benefit of feudalistic laws.

Until quite recently, there was little change in the brainwashing techniques through which the Party intended to purge the country of "parasitic Buddhist monks," "reactionary Christians" and all sorts of "imperialistic running dogs" masquerading in religious garb. Occasionally, in prisons and in labor camps, inmates participated in "accusation meetings," followed by long "political awareness raising sessions." At the end of these "mutual improvement sessions," they were expected "to surrender their hearts to the Party." Such a vigorous process is all-consuming. Some went mad, others committed suicide. Others again were converted. To someone like this author, who knows from personal experience, none of this is strange or banal. And he wants emphatically not to judge.

As Bishop Moser soon found out, many longterm Catholic prisoners had been released only to be put in a rural labor camp. It is not clear whether this means an improvement in their condition as their food ration is now tied to their production quota. A normal pace of work means, in certain cases and particularly with elderly people, slow starvation, while working to the limits of one's endurance means exhaustion.

Lately, Bishop Moser was told, conditions in labor camps have improved, and occasionally short visits to families are permitted. One priest who recently came out on a one-day leave was asked whether he would not prefer to leave the camp and the country. To which he unhesitatingly replied: "Why leave? There is no better place for me to serve my country and my Church. I'm doing pastoral work. I'm happy!"

Small wonder then that Bishop Moser returned to Germany with mixed feelings on what he had seen and heard. But as he kept saying very cautiously: "A beginning has been made."

Chapter 8:

The Vatican and the People's Republic of China

In the afterglow of Bishop Moser's visit, I should now like to say something about the relations of the Vatican and the PRC, a subject which has been the fertile ground of endless debate and speculation.

The best I can do is to give some elements of this debate and put some flesh on the dry bones of that speculation at the hand of what has been said and written during the last several months by authors who sometimes make the impression that they have the right answers to the wrong questions.

It would be tempting to write a thumbnail sketch of all the events, before and since the Communist takeover in 1949, which led up to the 1979 situation of relations between the PRC and the Vatican. But this is unnecessary because most of my readers are acquainted with the books of Bush, Laurentin, MacInnis, Patterson and Wei, as well as with more recent material   found in Whitehead and Concilium. American readers will find a short exposé by Sister Virginia Thérèse Johnson, M.M., in Worldmission, Summer 1976. Sister's article is entitled "Vatican-Peking Relations in this Time of Transition." In the light of subsequent events, this title strikes me as prophetic.

In 1979, every day was China day; every day was transition day! In Church&China relations, August was transition month. Unfortunately, at this writing, we are none the wiser on which direction transition will take. Now, goods in transit may never arrive; then, they may also show up very unexpectedly.

So let me start with August, or rather with the last days of July. On July 25, Msgr. Fu Tieshan, 48, was elected Bishop of Beijing at the 3rd enlarged meeting of the Beijing Patriotic Catholic Association. He succeeds Bishop Yao

Guangyu who died in 1964. The election was announced on
July 26 by Xinghua. The young bishop-elect said a first
solemn Mass on August 4 with 230 Catholics attending. He
celebrated Mass again on August 15, Feast of the Assumpti-
on, when 400 people were present, among them 32 foreigners.

On August 3, Msgr Panciroli, of the Vatican Press Bureau,
declared that "the Holy Father did not authorize, let alone
approve of, the election." On August 19, this provoked an
angry retort by mouth of the General Secretary of the Patriotic Association, Mr. Tang Lidao:

> We denounce the Vatican's blatant interference in the
> internal affairs of churches in other countries... The
> power of nominating bishops directly comes from God. The
> voice of the people is the voice of God.

As if by coincidence, on the same day, Pope John-Paul II
struck a conciliatory note during his Angelus Message at
Castelgandolfo. This message reverberated throughout the
world. This is what the Pope said:

> Our prayer is directed to God, constantly, for the great
> Chinese people, numerically the largest of the whole
> world. Only a limited part of the sons and daughters
> of that people was able in the past to welcome the tea-
> ching of Christ. In the year 1949, the Chinese Catholics
> were more than three million and the hierarchy numbered
> about one hundred bishops, of whom about forty were na-
> tive Chinese. There were five thousand eight hundred
> priests, of whom two thousand seven hundred were Chinese.
> It was a living Church, which maintained perfect union
> with the Apostolic See. After thirty years, the news
> that we have had about these brothers of ours is very
> little and uncertain. We do not cease, however, to nou-
> rish the hope to be able to establish once again with
> them that direct contact which spiritually was never
> interrupted. In fact, those who because of the lack
> of the possibility of visible relationship might have
> seemed absent, have never ceased to be present in a
> particular way in our prayers.

> We wish to do everything possible, so that the memory
> and the care which the Catholic community in the modern
> world nurtures for them, may lead to a drawing closer
> and eventually to a meeting. It is difficult to say
> anything on this matter. However, certain reports
> about recent events, which can make one think that
> there is a new respect with regard to religion, allow
> us to express some new confidence. With all my heart,
> I express the wish that there can be positive develop-
> ments, which for our brothers and sisters of the contin-
> ent of China may be the sign of the possibility of en-
> joying full religious liberty. (OR, 8/27:2)

The Pope's words were picked up by the world press and called "a major diplomatic gesture." An authoritative Vatican source called the Pontiff's statement "a major diplomatic initiative directed, not only to the Chinese Catholics, but also to Beijing's Communist government." It was, indeed, the first time that Pope John-Paul II spoke out on the Church in China.

Bishop Fu also reacted, reportedly with these words:

> Diplomatic relations between China and the Vatican are not only possible but desirable if the Vatican does not interfere with the internal affairs of the country. It is for the Vatican to recognize the independence of the Chinese Catholic Church. Until this happens, there is no room for dialogue with the Vatican on religious matters.

At least such is the version given by Le Monde on August 25. Other news sources, such as La Liberté of August 21 and La Croix of August 22, as well as The Tablet of September 1, reported things somewhat differently. According to these papers, Tang Lidao would have said:

> The Chinese Patriotic Church does not reject the Pope's appear out of hand, but a number of problems remain to be ironed out. Among these problems are: the right of Chinese Catholics to choose their own bishops independently from Rome; recognition of the Patriotic character of the Chinese Church; and the right of Catholics to take an independent stand on questions of international politics.

I also learned from another source that Bishop Fu had said: "I feel happy with the Pope's declaration." He is also quoted as having said that he would promote friendship with foreign Christians "on the basis of equality and mutual respect for each other's independence." (CT,12:5)

Bishop Fu is the leader of the Nantang community of priests since 1976. We are fairly well informed about this community which consists of 14 priests not all of whom board at the Cathedral. Among them, we mention Bishop Fu, ordained in 1956, Fathers Shi Yukun, 50, ordained in 1955, Niu Shengkui, 55, ordained in 1948, Sun Shangen, 52, who was ordained in 1956.

Friends who have met Bishop Fu describe him as an amiable and articulate person, chainsmoking in the presence of his guests. When interviews take place through an interpreter, it is obviously difficult to catch the inner meaning of words. A friend who met Bishop Fu recently reports after a pleasant conversation: "I know what I hear, but I do not know what he says."

Fu Tieshan had made the news at an earlier date. In December 1976, he reportedly told a U.S. News Service correspondent that he loved the late Mao Zedong more than God because Mao "stopped our suffering and changed the whole of China." No doubt, a clerical boutade! The same correspondent adds that while Fu remains celibate, celebrates the pre-Vatican II Tridentine Latin Mass, administers Holy Communion and hears confessions, he totally accepts divorce and abortion and insists that the Vatican -- to which he vows allegiance -- "has always been a tool of imperialism." (Robert J. Johnston in Commonweal, June 24, 1977, p. 394)

Again, in June, Fu told Philippe de Bausset: "The Vatican has incited the Christians and priests in China to fight against the government." After the usual tirade against the Gang of Four, Father Fu continued: "Each diocese must run its own affairs. Moreover, all bishops are equal, and the true successors of the Apostles. You are aware that we have our own point of view about the primacy of the Pope."(LF,6/22)

If I be permitted an innocent intermezzo at this point, let me remind the reader of the unreliability of some of our information, and of the difficulty of interpreting correctly the signs of the time, particularly as they surface in that immensely diverse country which is the PRC. In illustration, let me translate a paragraph from an article by Hans-Wolfgang Hessler which appeared in Evangelische Kommentare, January 1980, p. 20-3, under the title: "Christians in the Middle Kingdom: The Chances for the Church in China":

The Vatican Church-diplomacy does not conceal the fact that it foresees quick progress in its relations with the Middle Kingdom. Rome had hoped that Hua Guofeng would have visited the Vatican in October 1979 at the occasion of his trip to Europe. But the fact that he did not call upon the Pope has in no way been seen as a setback.

Little gestures tell much about the preparedness on either side to come to an understanding, even though both partners intend to get the most out of the bargain. Thus, the Vatican is showing flexibility in the matter of Taiwan. On the Chinese side, there is an effort at reconciliation related to the canonical problems around the consecration and function of newly elected bishops. Quite unexpectedly, the consecration of the new bishop of Beijing, Fu Tieshan, has been indefinitely postponed.

Not quite correct! Bishop Fu was consecrated on December 21 at a two and one-half hour consecration service in the Nantang, at which 400 persons were present, many of them in their late teens.

The consecration was duly announced by Xinhua on December
20, through the medium of an interview with Bishop Yang Gao-
jian "on the Chinese Catholic Church," which I quote in full:

> Monsignor Michael Yang Gaojian from the Changde diocese
> of Hunan said today he "accepted with great pleasure"
> the invitation to preside over the consecration cere-
> mony for Michael Fu Tieshan as bishop of Beijing, sche-
> duled tomorrow.
>
> The date coincides with the feast of St. Thomas, one of
> Jesus' 12 apostles who was said to have been to India
> and China.
>
> He will be joined by Bishop Louis Zhang Jiashu from the
> Shanghai diocese and bishop Francis Wang Xueming from
> the Hohhot diocese.
>
> The 66-year-old Bishop Yang said: "I am really glad,
> Michael Fu Tieshan is young and energetic. His virtue
> and knowledge has won him the respect of clergymen and
> Catholics in the Beijing diocese."
>
> He pointed out that no one had succeeded Monsignor
> Joseph Yao Guangyu in the Beijing diocese when he died
> in 1964. The consecration of Fu Tieshan has been long
> awaited.
>
> "His consecration is also a manifestation of the indepen-
> dence of the Chinese Catholic Church," Bishop Yang said,
> "which stands for self-administration, self-evangelism
> and self-support."
>
> "Religious authority is given by God and the voice of
> the people is the voice of God," he stressed.
>
> Bishop Yang is a national committee member of the Chin-
> ese People's Political Consultative Conference and was
> Deputy Secretary-General to the All-China Patriotic
> Catholic Association since its establishment in 1957.
>
> Chinese Catholics began to elect and consecrate their
> own bishops in 1958 and have since ordained over 50
> bishops. Monsignor Yang was one of them.
>
> By contrast, over 90% of the bishops in China before
> the founding of the People's Republic of China in 1949
> were foreigners.
>
> Catholicism was introduced to China in 1582. Michael
> Fu Tieshan will be Beijing's third Chinese bishop in
> the 379 years since Catholicism was introduced to Bei-
> jing in 1601.

"We were deprived of our right to succeed the apostles of Jesus in old China," Monsignor Yang said, "and we gained our independence only after new China was founded. We treasure it."

He says he was afraid of the Communist Party when Liberation came in 1949. A native of Hunan, he was brought up in a Catholic family and began to study theology at the age of 12. He was ordained priest in 1938 after he graduated from a seminary in Wuhan, Hubei, and returned to his hometown to do missionary work.

"The Communist Party and the Liberation Army proved that they really cared for the people. When I saw how the people improved their lives and saw their confidence in the country and in themselves growing, I felt hopeful, and I became willing to take an active part in the Patriotic Movement against imperialism and for socialism in China," he said.

As a leader of the All-China Patriotic Catholic Association, Bishop Yang said the organisation aimed at assisting the government to implement the national policy of freedom of religious belief. "Its present task is to unite clergymen and the members of the Church to win modernization for China under the leadership of the government," he said.

"It's our obligation as citizens of the People's Republic of China," he said.

All religious activities stopped during the Cultural Revolution. Clergymen were persecuted by the Gang of Four.

"The government policy on religion came back to life after the downfall of the Gang of Four," Bishop Yang said. "We have faith in it."

The bishop listed the Church's urgent tasks: training young priests; setting up a seminary, the preparation of which was under way in the 1960's and interrupted by the Cultural Revolution; republishing the quarterly "Dove of Faith."

He regarded his position in the Consultative Conference as "a bridge between Catholics and the government." "I pass on to Church members government policies and make their wishes known to the government," he said.

Perhaps more than any other recent document, the statement by Bishop Yang clarifies the situation of the Catholic Patriotic Church, and gives us a glimpse of its plans for the future.

At the Vatican, the Pope too had received the news of Bishop Fu's consecration on December 21. In his annual allocution to the Cardinals at the occasion of Christmas on December 22, the Holy Father specifically referred to China in that part of his discourse which described the "true dimensions of religious liberty." He said in part:

> In many countries the true dimensions of religious liberty do not exist. It is difficult to understand, for example, how the concept of scientific and social development can be considered bound up with the imposition of an atheistic program today...

> The Church should be able to carry out her mission under every sky, in respect of mutual freedoms but also in the performance of her own indefeasable rights, as they are proclaimed in the Gospel.

> In this connection my thought returns with special affection to the great Chinese people, whom I already recalled on Sunday 19 August of this year, at the recitation of the Angelus. As Christmas draws near, I send my greeting and my good wishes to the sons of the Catholic Church, as to all the members of that great nation, renewing "the hope that there may be positive developments, which will mark for our brothers and sisters of the Chinese continent the possibility of enjoying full religious freedom. (OR, Jan. 14, 1980)

According to the radio broadcast which summarized the Pope's speech that evening, the Holy Father digressed at this point from his prepared text and described to the Cardinals what had happened the day before in Beijing. He then concluded: "I feel profoundly hurt."

+

+ +

+

As I have done in the case of Islam, Buddhism and Protestantism, I shall now give the full text of an address on the Catholic Church by Mr Tang Lidao at the occasion of the Japanese Buddhist group's visit to Beijing in April 1974. We know already that Mr Tang, who is a layman, occupies the important post of General Secretary of the Catholic Patriotic Association. In this capacity he met with Bishop Moser and is the official spokesman for his constituency. This is what he told his Buddhist visitors:

> We welcome Mr Niwano and his companions to China. We strongly believe that this visit will promote mutual goodwill and understanding. The Catholics are in total

agreement with what the other representatives here have said. As for me, I should like to add something on the relations between the Chinese Catholic Church and the Vatican.

In the past, China fell victim to the inroads of imperialism. Many missionaries came to our country. Many Catholics fell into hell, by which I mean that they protected the interests of imperialism and in many ways also of colonialism. The Catholic Church became the instrument of the invasion of China, and the Vatican upheld this state of affairs and encouraged it. The Vatican thereby became also guilty of the crimes of imperialism and of the invasion of our country.

After our liberation, Catholics went underground and are reported still to plot the ruin of China. The Vatican has issued orders for the destruction of movements of justice in our country. This made it necessary for Chinese Catholics to establish their independence from the Vatican. The Vatican continues its inimical policy towards China and threatens with the heaviest penalty for those who do not obey, namely the penalty of excommunication.

In 1958, an antirevolutionary faction arose in Shanghai. (This is an allusion to Bishop Kong Pingmei's resistance to the government.) Later bishops were chosen by the people. The Vatican resented this patriotic action, and praised the bishop who had led the antirevolutionary activities about which I spoke. The Vatican looked askance at all patriotic activities and called them a shame. The Catholic Church of China, however, has now been educated by the struggle of the last 20 years. Through an intense personal experience, we have come to realize that our relations with the Vatican are not religious relations.

The key point is that the Vatican has continued a strategy which is detrimental to China. We know that John XXIII and Paul VI took steps to renew the Church. However, these are only meant to deceive. We constantly hear sayings such as "Each religion must face reality, so let us forget the past," or again, "Let us extinguish the rancor of the past, and let us turn together against our common enemies."

I ask you, what is one to think of that? Personally, I think that such gestures are anti-revolutionary and anti-socialist. Their reactionary nature has not changed a bit. Hence we shall continue to protect the independence of our Church. We shall continue to oppose the interference of the Vatican. We shall win the battle for justice!

Six years after this speech, Mr Tang, as far as I know, still speaks vigorously for the Patriotic Church. He now has a modest office, but as yet no staff. It is his duty to forward to visitors who apply the certificate for permission by the Beijing Municipal Office to visit the remains of Archbishop Pi Shushi who was buried among other heroes of the Revolution in the cemetery of Paopaoshan. The Archbishop became, after some years in prison, the President of the Patriotic Association and a member of the National Assembly. His remains can be reverenced in Room 10, No. 94. It will be recalled that, at Pi's funeral in May 1978, a colleague of his, Mr Zhao Puchu, the General Secretary of the All-China Buddhist Association who was at Princeton (p. 74), pronounced the eulogy. We do not know, however, whether a religious ceremony took place at that occasion

But let us get back to the Patriotic Church. Several standard reasons have been given by the Chinese authorities for the impossibility of normalizing relations with the Vatican. Bishop Moser heard them all from the mouth of Bishop Fu. Here are the usual main three reasons:

-- There are no diplomatic relations between the Vatican and China. This, in Chinese eyes, seems to be a crucial affair. Its roots go back to the expulsion of Archbishop Riberi, and invariably bring up the contentious nature of the Vatican's diplomatic relations with Taiwan. This is a vast subject with which I cannot possibly deal in this book. I can only make room for the most recent and most authoritative declaration on the matter as voiced by Premier Hua Guofeng at his press conference in Beijing on October 7, in preparation for his trip to Europe.

Piero Ostellino, correspondent of the <u>Corriere della Sera</u> asked this question: "Recently people have talked a lot about dialogue between China and the Vatican. What are the prospects for the relations between the two countries? Do you intend to meet the Pope this time?"

Hua answered: "There are no contacts between China and the Vatican. I am going to Italy on an official visit. I have no plan whatsoever of meeting with people in the Vatican, the Pope or other personnel from there. I want to add that the Vatican still has relations with the Kuomintang in Taiwan, which has a so-called ambassador there. In these circumstances, we cannot consider coming into any contact with the Vatican. (<u>BR</u>, 10/12:11)

-- The former entanglement of the Church with colonial powers.

-- The indecision among Mao's successors about the degree of freedom which they can afford to give without endangering the regime.

Obviously, there are other reasons of a more personal nature.
The Vatican might want to know more about the Patriotic Church
and its officials, particularly its bishops, before confirming
them. In this respect, the recent visits of Msgr Chao, Michael
Chu, and Bishop Moser, as far as I know, had few practical results, particularly because none of them had free access to all
the people they wished to meet.

It is not so much the canonical niceties which clamor for
attention, nor the fact that the Vatican would be unwilling
to bend over backwards trying to do full justice to the Chinese
situation, it is the rockbottom fact that no organization can
call itself "Catholic" without a mutually accepted bond with
Rome, i.e., with the Pope.

At the end of December, the situation had hardly improved.
Bishop Fu said Christmas Mass in his cathedral before a record
congregation of 800 people, many of them Chinese. Last year,
during Christmas Mass, TV cameras were in action, but nothing
appeared on the screen.

+

+   +

+

It is natural that, particularly since August, visitors to
China as well as theologians of note have rushed in where
angels fear to tread. Each one of them comes up with his own
diagnostic, and his own nostrums for a cure. Here I can only
mention some of the more prominent names who publicly discussed the issue, and let them talk for themselves.

1. Father Louis Wei, 77, was born in Shanghai but has lived
   in Paris for the last forty years. Wei is well-known for
two books and numerous articles which, some feel, are not
without considerable bias against the Vatican. Be that as it
may, Father Wei travelled for the second time to China on an
extended "voyage nostalgique" (as he puts it) of one hundred
days. When he returned to Hong Kong at the beginning of October 1978, we had dinner together, and I was able to hear
from him some of his brand-new impressions.

Or perhaps not so new. Father Wei has, for many years,
put much of the blame for the bad relations between China
and the Vatican in the shoes of the successor to the Fisher-
man. He likes to discourse for hours on "the ambiguous
politics of the Vatican vis-à-vis China," the title of an
angry article which he published in Le Monde, September 16,
1975.

Recently, Father Wei charged again with another article
in Le Figaro, September 1, 1979, entitled "l'Enigme de la
politique du Vatican." A few months earlier, he had talked
at great length to Claude-François Jullien in an interview
which led to a sensational "Document de la Semaine" in Le
Nouvel Observateur of April 9. Louis Wei makes his points
with total conviction, at least to himself. He is a man
with wide connections; he corresponds with Bishop Fu Tieshan; he told me that he had been given by the Beijing
authorities "highly incriminating documents," which he is
preparing for publication.

Hence, I feel, Father Wei has many things of interest to
tell, and he should be listened to before he slips away on
another trip to China in March 1980, for which he is now
raising the necessary funds. From his Hong Kong conversation and the other documents which I mentioned, here are
some details of note:

> The bishops of the Patriotic Church are waiting for the
> tide to turn; they are waiting for the dialogue between
> the Vatican and Beijing to start. Bishops seldom meet.
> In Beijing no one knew about the death of Bishop Tang
> although he died close by. Bishop Chang Qiashu of Shang-
> hai was elected by the clergy in succession to Bishop
> Kong Pingmei, condemned to life imprisonment in 1955.
> Kong is still in prison but enjoys a special treatment.
> Bishop Chang, with all other bishops and Catholics say
> that "they are in communion with the Holy See, but in
> total disagreement with the China policy of the Vatican."

> My sister with whom I stayed wanted to have me say Mass.
> At four in the morning, I slipped into her room and
> celebrated Mass with rice and tea. I had to make haste
> because at 4.30 AM everybody must get up. China is an
> immense monastery where everybody, also priests, observe
> four vows: obedience, poverty, chastity and stability,
> much like the Benedictine monks. The seven Catholics who
> came to my Mass in Beijing told me: "There is no way of
> handing on the faith to others. Our children would not
> understand. To them our faith is antirevolutionary.
> Moreover, no one is allowed to practice a religion be-
> fore age 18.

> Some bishops have been consecrated since 1958. Of the
> 45 of them, 30 are still alive. Two are in prison be-
> cause they were not patriotic enough. In the central
> provinces, there still may be bishops appointed by
> Rome, but I am not sure. There still are Catholics in
> China, but if Rome doesn't change its policy, they will
> disappear.

The Vatican has worked out its Ostpolitik to re-establish relations with the East bloc. Why not do something
similar for China? That will even be more difficult.
Propaganda Fide will always object. But its mission is
finished. We must let the Chinese evangelize China.
Rome must take the first step, close its Nunciature in
Taiwan, and send Archbishop Casaroli to China. Meanwhile the Church in China, which is an invisible, pre-
Constantinian Church, suffers and dies.

Father Wei concludes his Le Figaro article with this parting shot: "The Church in China looks for candidates to the
episcopacy. About one hundred bishops will be elected and
consecrated in the coming months." That, I submit, might
not be of much help toward a solution.

2. Père René Laurentin is a theologian of international re-
pute, a highly respected journalist, and a scholar who
is best known in China circles for his book Chine et Christianisme: Après les occasions manquées, 1977.

In Le Figaro of October 17, Laurentin takes on where Père
Wei leaves off and returns to the possibility of non-canon-
ical episcopal consecrations in the near future. And he
comments on this possibility:

> If such elections of bishops took place without Rome's
> consent, then we shall be witnessing an event as terri-
> ble, even perhaps more terrible, than the schism between
> East and West in 1054, a schism which has not yet been
> healed notwithstanding the Ecumenical Council and a
> deep yearning for reunion on both sides. Time is not
> on the side of those who want to heal schisms. Shall
> the new Pope be able to abandon those sterile timidities
> which have allowed the Church-and-China gap to deepen
> for more than a quarter century?

> Does the Church realize the gravity of the situation,
> and the historical deadweight of this problem? Shall
> she be able to come up with something new, because the
> relations between Chinese and Christians must take off
> from new grounds?

> No return to the past! This is the conclusion of all
> the China meetings which have been held during the last
> ten years by Christians with a passionate love and an
> admiration for the noble and pacific Chinese people,
> for their attention to the common good, to community,
> sacrifice, and the exacting moral standards which they
> have set for themselves. Mr Hua Guofeng will visit
> Italy, a country which has been more eager to establish
> amicable relations with China than France. It is

customary for a visiting Chief of State to call upon
the Pope while in Rome. It is said that Mr Hua shall
not see the Pope. Is this really a hopeless case?
Shall we never succeed in eliminating the European
mythologies about the Chinese and the Chinese mythologies about the Christians? These mythologies still
plague us long after I have denounced them in my book.

Laurentin then finishes with this arresting thought:

A summit meeting could become the venue of a daring
initiative. Such an initiative would give the lie to
that bureaucratic lethargy of which both the Vatican
and China sometimes have been accused. The stakes are
very high. More than appears, the future of the world
and of peace hangs in the balance.

Premier Hua, indeed, came to Rome, and he did not see the
Pope. Although I was not surprised, I was deeply saddened
at what Laurentin would call another "occasion manquée."
With Laurentin's "daring initiative" in my head I went to
bed. I had a dream. I dreamed that the Pope was on his
way to Japan in the Fall of 1980 when the maple trees dress
up the country in the gorgeous reddish-yellow kimono of
their leaves. It so happened that, for technical reasons
(as they say), the Pope's plane was forced to stop for re-
fuelling at Beijing. What a surprise for me to see in the
reception line such famous Catholic visitors as Bishop
Moser, Prince Jean of Luxembourg, King Baldwin of the Belgians (who is scheduled to go to China this coming June)
and Hans Küng... I counted about 200 Catholics on the
apron, led by Bishop Fu Tieshan who wore his episcopal
robes and the pectoral cross which he inherited from Archbishop Pi Shushi.

The Pope came down the gangplank dressed in his red cape.
He was followed by Cardinal Casaroli, reportedly the brains
behind the Vatican's Ostpolitik, who wore a black cassock.
Premier Hua, Vice-premier Deng, Foreign Minister Huang Hua
and the mayor of Beijing emerged from the gleaming-new airport lounge reserved for VIP's. When the mayor introduced
himself, the Pope answered much the same way as he had already done in New York: "Mr Mayor, while I'm in the capital,
I'll try to be a good citizen." There were smiles all
around and nothing else was said. Without further ado, the
dignitaries climbed in their limousines and drove off towards the city.

Scattered crowds had gathered along the wide thoroughfares
which lead to the Temple of Heaven. Not knowing too well
for whom, they waved little Chinese flags. Premier Hua
apologized to the Pope: "Your visit was so unexpected that

we had no time to hand out Vatican flags. The Pope didn't
mind. Vaguely remembering a saying of Chairman Mao, he
said: "Mr Premier, it's not the flags that count, it's the
people." Hua nodded in agreement.

The police had reserved an open space on the Terrace of
Heaven for the Catholics of Beijing. It is there that, since
the fifteenth century, the Ming and Qing emperors yearly
came to offer the solemn sacrifice of propitiation for the
sins of the people. I quickly counted some 2000 Catholics,
all fingering their rosaries, and singing at the top of
their voices "Tsai-tien wo-men fu-chi 在天我們父者 , Our
Father who are in heaven." In the front row of this jubil-
ant crowd, I remarked the twenty priests from Ya-er street.
They looked as if they were in a daze. Some of them had not
left their residence for more than 15 years.

When the cortège arrived at the Temple of Heaven, the Pope
so quickly mounted the steps that the dignitaries had trouble
keeping up with him. When he arrived at the highest plane
from where only heaven can be seen, the Pope dropped on his
knees and kissed the ground. The Chinese interpreted this
gesture as a sign of reverence for their people, its glorious
past and its recent achievements. They also saw it as a
sign of reconciliation between China and the Church. There
was a discreet round of applause from the Chinese leaders.

Before the Pope could be asked to go and see some of the
newly opened churches, or even shake hands with any of the
Catholics, he had vanished and was not seen again until he
arrived in Tokyo. Cardinal Casaroli was not with him.

This is just a dream. But is it an impossible dream?

3. Père Marie-Dominique Chenu, O.P., is another theologian
   of great renown, appreciated for the pastoral insights
as well as the missionary importance of his work. (On Chenu,
I recommend the fine pages of Yves Congar in R. Vander
Gucht and H. Vorgrimler, ed., Bilan de la Théologie du XXe
Siècle, Paris: Casterman, 1970) Chenu speaks directly to
the problem of the Patriotic Church in an article of Le
Monde, August 21, titled "First the Gospel, then the Institution." He mentions newspaper accounts of Bishop Fu Tieshan's appointment and the Vatican's reaction. He feels
that certain ambiguities need clearing up. To that effect,
he tells this petite anecdote:

   Monsignor Van Melckebeke, a bishop of Dutch nationality
   (Excuse me, Père Chenu, Bishop Van Melckebeke is Belgian,
   a confrère of mine and a friend.), who previously worked
   in China for some thirty years, was forced to leave the

country about the year 1950. Since that time he has continued to serve the many Chinese communities in the diaspora of South-East Asia. While in Rome for the Council in 1962, the bishop went to see Pope John XXIII and told him: "Your Holiness, at diverse occasions you have strongly spoken out against those Catholic bishops in China who do their work without your consent. They refuse all contact with the bishop of Rome and hence they find themselves somehow in a state of schism. Those bishops, Your Holiness, I know them one by one, and I assure you that they are fine priests. And they are right in not wanting to have any contact with you. In China, the Pope is considered to be the worst of all western "imperialist potentates" who for centuries have oppressed China, not only economically and politically, but culturally as well. From the West, this seems to be preposterous, and yet such a stand expresses the common feelings of the Chinese government which are the tragic carry-over from the past."

Indeed, without even mentioning the confusion between missionaries and colonial powers, the Roman Church has condemned during six centuries the worship of ancestors as "idolatry." This worship is at the very heart of Chinese religiosity. It remains the basis of that astonishing sense of community which distinguishes the Chinese people. Only after 1940 did the Church recognize that she had erred.

At this point, Père Chenu has Bishop Van Melckebeke continue:

Your Holiness, if therefore a bishop keeps his distance, the reason is that, to exercise his ministry, it is essential for him to be accepted by the people and by the authorities. Otherwise he can do nothing. Now, the Gospel comes first, and then the Institution.

When the Pope heard these words from such a qualified and experienced man, he wept and said: "Come back in another month, and repeat what you have said." As soon as the Council session ended, Pope John publicly rejected the word schism. Since that day, nor he nor his successors, even when they expressed their sorrow at the situation, have ever used that word again. To the contrary, they have never missed an opportunity to speak about "the signs of a new situation."

I have this tale from Msgr Van Melckebeke himself. More details can be read in Père Laurentin's book, p. 186-92.

Thus far Père Chenu. Let me add at this point something

which is not found in Laurentin. I have been told that,
before the opening of Vatican II, a consultation took place
between Pope John, Cardinal Tardini, the Secretary of State,
and Archbishop Sigismondi of Propaganda. The question was
asked: Should uncanonically consecrated Chinese bishops
be invited to participate in the Council. Cardinal Tardini
convinced the Pope that an invitation was not appropriate.
The Pope reluctantly agreed, and wept.

Père Chenu concludes with these words:

> It is opportune to call to mind what Msgr Van Melckebeke
> has said when confronted with the awkward comments in
> the press, even the religious press. Better still, this
> anecdote tells us much about the need sharply to distin-
> guish between the Gospel preached to the poor and the
> Institution. History must be followed closely because
> evolution goes on beyond the juridical and diplomatic
> niceties. René Laurentin puts this very well: " We must
> renounce our western ethnocentrism and look at China
> with new eyes and with an open mind. We must look at
> China for her own sake, and not as if she were a field
> of action and a zone opened to our influence. We must
> want to be challenged by this fact which has become a
> sign of hope among the younger generation and in the
> whole Third World."

For Church-and-China, to be able and willing to do what
Laurentin and Chenu suggest, this too looks like a dream.
But is it an impossible dream?

4. Hans Küng is the internationally famous professor at
   Tübingen University. In early September Küng went to
China, ably assisted by his interpreter, Sinologist Julia
Ching. After his trip, he gave a lecture in Hong Kong de-
scribing his impressions. A summary of this lecture is found
in Asia Lutheran News, Hong Kong, August-September. Later
Küng also was interviewed by a German broadcasting station:

> He stated that in his opinion the interest that the
> People's Republic of China is now showing in religion
> is honest. Prof. Küng had taken part in Beijing in the
> official meeting between the Chinese Academy for Science
> and the Kennedy Institute of Ethics in Washington. On
> this occasion the question of religion was debated open-
> ly for the first time in communist China.

> Even if the interest of the state in religions is poli-
> tically motivated, and one should not be too optimistic,
> Küng felt it a positive sign that there is now an Insti-
> tute for the Study of World Religions within the Academy
> of Science, that a modern translation of the Bible is
> being prepared and that the churches are open again.

Küng foresees great difficulties with regard to an arrangement between the Holy See and the Catholic Patriotic People's Church, particularly because of the Chinese
demand for self-government by the churches. Speaking of
the recent election of the Bishop of Beijing without
agreement from Rome, Küng pointed to the inflexible attitude of the Catholic Church on elections of bishops, but
felt that a solution would be possible since "in former
times bishops in the Catholic Church were always chosen
locally and any agreement from Rome -- if it was indeed
asked for -- was obtained after the event. (KIPA, 9/16)

Küng's solution, as he intimates, would require major changes in Church policy, and such changes would have to sustain
the scrutiny, not only of scriptural and historical theological research, but, equally important, of their pastoral ac-
ceptability, not only by Rome, but also by the people involved.

5. Monsignor Pietro Chao is a priest born in Manchuria. At
present he is dean of mission studies in the Urbanianum
University and in charge of Vatican Radio programs in Chinese.
Hence he is well known to the Chinese authorities. He arrived
in China from Hong Kong on November 6, 1978, and returned
there on December 27. He visited twelve major cities, and
wherever he went, he was received with unusual courtesy.

The foreign press showed considerable interest in Msgr
Chao's visit to his homeland. At best, we can only sample
the mass of information which it brought forth. Thus Le
Monde, March 17, feels inclined to write:

> Articles in the People's Daily lead to conjecture that
> the possibility of normalizing the situation of the Chi-
> nese Catholic Church has been discussed in Beijing. Such
> a possibility, it would seem, was the reason for the
> trip of a Vatican representative, Msgr Pietro Chao, to
> China. He is the first envoy of Rome to the PRC in
> twenty years. His trip has been shrouded in extreme
> discretion, and the results are unknown.

It is rumored that Msgr Chao has prepared a report on his
trip but that he prefers to keep it confidential. Le Monde
continues:

> Observers feel that one of the thorniest problems which
> may have been discussed at Beijing is the fate of Chinese
> members of religious orders who are still in the country
> but who did not join "patriotic" organizations." Only to
> mention the Jesuits , about 100 of them are dispersed
> throughout the country. Some of them are still under
> arrest, others are working at different jobs, e.g., as

translators. Should normalization become a fact, shall
these religious men and women then be forced to join the
Patriotic Organizations? Could the Vatican recognize
a Chinese church from which priests loyal to its authority would be excluded?

The answer to this poignant question is obvious. Unfortunately it is an obvious Yes to Beijing, and an equally
obvious No to Rome. Fortunately, in the difficult and ambiguous circumstances in which we live, nothing, in Beijing or
in Rome, is as obvious as it seems. Meanwhile, Le Monde concludes, not much has changed. Unfortunately, this is correct

+

+   +

+

The Jesuits in China have just been mentioned. In 1979,
nothing has shown the thirstiness for good news among Catholics, and nothing has brought them such a proleptic joy at
a possible renewal of relations with the Vatican as the
canard that "the Jesuits have been invited to reopen Aurora
University in Shanghai." Here are the bare facts of this
year's "Chinese spring":

Newspapers, like Le Monde on January 23 and March 21, say
that the PRC would like to reopen the Aurora University in
Shanghai, formerly under the direction of the Jesuit Fathers.
The university was founded by them in 1903 and closed by the
Chinese authorities in July 1951. Since 1908, the rules of
the University specified that "religion is not the matter"
(as far as educational policy is concerned).

To add piquancy to the news, it was said that "former professors would be welcome." Obviously, these Jesuits would be
in their seventies by now. On March 19, Father Arrupe, General of the Society of Jesus, expressed the readiness of his
men to accept the offer. This announcement came over radio
and TV; it generated great rejoicing throughout the Catholic
world. But the joy was short-lived as the French Embassy in
Beijing, which presumably had bruited the news of an invitation to the Jesuits, issued a démenti. Indeed, the new version reads, mention had been made of the French taking over
a Chinese university, but not necessarily the Aurora.

Then there was a new flurry of encouraging news as Le Monde excitedly announced that "a Chinese Jesuit would be allowed to visit his homeland as a religious." (6/21) The Vatican Fides News Agency, 6/19, had indeed informed the world
that the Jesuit's name was Father Michael Chu, a priest born
in Shanghai from a long ancestry of prominent Catholics.

Father Chu, before being called to Rome as Assistant to the General, was his Society's provincial in Taiwan. Fides further specified: "Father Chu has received permission to visit his family, and particularly his aged mother. He will be staying in the PRC for some time." Chu would also want to contact, as much as possible, his Chinese confreres of whom reportedly 121 are still alive in China. None of these Jesuits exercise their priestly ministry in public. Many of them are collocated in work camps around the country.

Fides added a word of caution: "Although this trip seems to be a new sign of the thaw in relations between China and the outside world,its importance should not be exaggerated." In fact, this warning was prophetic. Father Chu remained in China for 70 days, 38 of them he spent in Shanghai, 12 in Chengde, a lovely city where the emperors' summer palaces are located, and 20 in Beijing. Five of his brothers were allowed to leave their workcamps for a short time, and visit with him.

No concrete results of Father Chu's trip have been revealed. Yet the Jesuits-for-China mood would not easily evaporate. At the occasion of Chu's trip, major newspapers ran long and enthusiastic articles on the most famous Jesuit ever to set foot in China, Matteo Ricci (Li Matou, 1552-1610). Even in Beijing, the People's Daily of November 4 chimed in and un-blushingly called Ricci "the greatest of all East-West scho-lars." (See cover) Le Matin, March 22 and June 19, ran a short history of the Ricci era. Le Monde, not to be out-written by its competitor, boldly advertized a perpetual bestseller, Lettres de Chine par des Missionnaires Jésuites, 1702-1776, Paris: Garnier-Flammarion.(June 1)

Previously, an opening salvo in the rash of Ricci praise had been sounded in Venice where Chinese and Italian schol-ars, in October 1978, met to discuss the scientific contri-butions to China by Ricci and his fellow Jesuits -- which is precisely the theme of the PD article on the cover of this book, an article which has nothing to say about his religious activities.

I have also spotted Ricci material from the pen of the Leibniz-and-China specialist David Mungello in CN, Summer 1978. Another article by John D. Young came out in CF, No. 2, 1979, comparing the Jesuit and the Protestant ap-proach to China. Finally, Léon Trivière, one of the best-informed scholars on Church-and-China, also joined the cho-rus with a well-researched article on "Les Jésuites en Chine" in the maiden issue of a literary and artistic magazine, Paris-Pékin, September-October.

SALVATION IS TO BE FOUND IN MAOIST CHINA

There is a level on which this proposition cannot be refuted within Christian theology. Since Creation and Redemption are not totally separate, since God is the God of all Creation, then China cannot be left out of God's Providence.

In this sense, White South Africa, the ruling classes of Chile and South Korea and North America, and all kinds of persons and groups are not totally separated from God's saving work.

The point here is different. It is based on an assessment of China which says that in the Maoist revolution to a significant extent justice is done and the broken are healed. Insofar as this is true, what Christians call God's saving power is there.

There are those who claim to disagree with this position on theological grounds. Charles West has said that it is idolatrous to identify God's salvation with any particular human movement. On these grounds the biblical writers are idolatrous. The liberation of the people of Israel from bondage in Egypt, a violent event in which Pharaoh's army was drowned, is interpreted by the biblical writers and rmembered by the people, as God's saving act. It is a prototype of Salvation referred to again and again in the entire Judeo-Christian tradition.

The principle here is more important than just the question of Maoism. We are called constantly to make decisions about political issues. To simply identify as God's will the causes we discern to be correct would be an error. Nevertheless, it is wrong also to say that such issues and decisions have nothing to do with salvation.

The Judeo-Christian tradition has always discovered salvific meaning in diverse human movements. There are no theological or biblical grounds for denying the possibility of salvific meaning in the Chinese revolution. The problem becomes one, then, of our very human and imperfect assessment of the political, cultural and social factors at work in that movement.

A last point is that the Chinese do have an implied "transcendent" of sorts. They talk of the inevitable laws of history which operate regardless of human will. These laws move peoples toward liberation and fulfillment. In a sense the Maoists live with the same necessary paradoxes as the Christians -- a person is morally responsible, yet there are forces at work over which one does not have control.

Raymond L. Whitehead in Whitehead, p. 231-49

CHRISTIANS IN CONVERSATION: THE SEARCH FOR HERMENEUTICS

A. There is concern over the split between the Patriotic and non-Patriotic Catholics. The question is how to bring these two groups together. If only the official representatives of the Patriotic Association are invited (to renew contacts), would this not widen the cleavage?

B. Both Catholics and Protestants in Hong Kong, if they care enough, can do much because they are closer. There is the problem of evaluating the cleavage which western missionary societies tend to exaggerate.

C. We can draw from the example of the situation in Eastern Europe. Outside interest can help start a discussion between the two groups. Experience shows that if left simply to themselves the cleavage will not improve.

D. K.H. Ting has sent a message to Peter Lee to inform him that the cleavage is not evident.

E. We do not know if the cleavage between the "official" and the "silent" churches is that great. In China, the silent church applies to Bishop Kong of Shanghai and other priests imprisoned up to now. However, it is important to keep in mind that Kong and those priests had a pre-Vatican TT theology. They were imprisoned not for their faith but for their "counter-revolutionary activities." For example Kong had advised Catholics on "3-don'ts" in their dealings with the Patriotic Movement: do not listen to or speak to the Patriotic Association and do not sign their statements. Kong did all he could to obstruct the movement. Whenever the government called a meeting he would also call one at the same time to respond to it, thus dividing the conscience of Catholics.

I went to China in 1978 and met two persons who had just attended a meeting of the Patriotic Association in Shanghai. They told me that Bishop Chang had given a report on the situation. It was said at the meeting that there were groups meeting in parks in the city for religious activities and that there were people giving out Bibles. They felt that this was because churches were not yet open and these people had no place to go for their worship. The persons I contacted cared not at all about the legitimacy of the official Church which is separated from the Vatican. Maybe they are not representative, but they are people who recite rosaries aloud in boats in public. They couldn't care less if they are recognized by Rome or not as long as they get their sacraments.

F. Priests in Hong Kong give a different version. Many Catholics did care, and many died or were imprisoned for not co-operating with the official church.

At the beginning of January, 1980, the excitement around Michael Chu's trip ha^d died out. As the days go by and more news filters out of China, it becomes evident that the problem of reconciliation among two groups of Chinese Catholics looms as perhaps the most impassable barrier on the way to an improvement of Vatican-PRC relations. Well-informed and well-meaning Christians are anxiously searching for elementary hermeneutics which would help them analyze a very difficult, explosive situation. (See p. 145) The watchword is, more than ever, extreme prudence in judging, extreme proficiency in learning all about a fluid situation, and extreme patience in planning for the future. Such are the 3 P's which mark any China-research worthy of theology, and worthy of the Chinese people.

Our anxiety, our sympathy, and our unflinching desire for mutual understanding embraces all Catholics without exception. Only God knows what those went through who did not join the Patriotic Church. And only God knows the hidden grief of those who joined, and yet were not spared physical harm under the Gang of Four, nor anguish and humiliation after their fall.

Only very recently did atheist members of the Bureau of Religions tell Monsignor Chang Qiashu, the "Patriotic Bishop" of Shanghai since 1960, that "the Constitution guarantees you religious freedom; there is no more need for you or your people to blaspheme your God; to the contrary, you may now pray and say Mass." That is exactly what the bishop did. On June 3, the Feast of Pentecost, he gathered his priests and sisters in a little chapel for Mass. They all made their public confession, after which the bishop gave them absolution. Similar little events happened throughout the country. Priests and bishops who have kept sofar their distance from the Patriotic Church have been tapped on the shoulder by the police and told of their constitutional freedom of religion. Hence, they need no longer remain under cover; they can now come forth and take charge of their local community.

I do not know whether any of them has accepted the outstretched hand. They have seen so much change; their hope has been betrayed so often. Perhaps they prefer to keep their peace, their joy, their faith, and die with dignity. They all know the proverb which says: "The problem is not the difficulty of the task but one's determination" 天下无难事、只怕有心人．

Chapter 9:

The daily life of Catholics

We have these words of Thomas Moore: "Eyes have no sorrow that Heaven cannot heal." Moore wrote about what he knew, as he paid with his life for what he believed. He was a most delightful man. He kept his sense of humor higher than the gallows on which he was beheaded. He never tried to save his head, only his innocent beard.

From a sheaf of reports on the daily life of Catholics in the PRC, a composite portrait vaguely emerges of which, I fancy, Thomas Moore would heartily approve. In their own inimitable way they put into practice that marvelous Chinese proverb: "You cannot prevent the birds from flying over your head, but you can prevent them from building nests in your hair."

And they too keep their sense of humor. Father Louis Wei told me in Hong Kong that, in the PRC, one should never mention the name of Archbishop Riberi because he remains "la bête noire des Chinois." Quite true. Communists remember the anti-Riberi campaign which climaxed in his perfunctory expulsion from China on September 5, 1951. The technical, communist name for this event is gexin 革新, which literally means "reform." Catholics also have their gexin, but they write it differently with these characters: 割心. Literally, this means "to cut the heart" and it implies that they would rather die than be disloyal to their faith.

Thomas Moore forgave his judges and bade their whole company au revoir in heaven. In a Catholic village of Manchuria, under the Cultural Revolution, two priests were buried alive. They belonged both to the diocese of Kirin. Their names are John the Baptist Xia Kuii, born in 1887 and ordained in 1915, and Francis Tin Shuting, also born in 1887 and ordained in 1911. Standing at the side of their graves both priests gave a stirring talk to the crowd. They forgave their executioners, some of whom converted. Their death brought greater unity to the local Catholics.

About the same time, on a June Sunday of 1950, Father
John Tong was dragged before a People's Court in Zhongqing
to the cries: "Down with the imperialist Riberi -- let the
government expel him!" About what happened then we have this
report:

> Ascending the speaker's rostrum, Tong traced on himself
> the sign of the Cross, and began, as all sermons preached
> in Catholic Churches begin, with the words, "In the name of
> the Father and of the Son and of the Holy Ghost." Then in
> the stillness as of a church he continued. The point that
> I wish to say is this: "I offer myself as a sacrificial
> victim to bring about an understanding between the gov-
> ernment and the Church."
>
> It is those very people, who deny the existence of God
> and of the immortal soul, who do not recognize the Vicar
> of Jesus Christ on earth -- the Holy Father -- and the
> position of the Hierarchy in relation to the Catholic
> Church, who would claim that the "Three Independencies"
> (self-government, self-support and self-propagation)
> movement is merely a patriotic movement. They profess
> the freedom of religion and admit the spiritual ties
> between believers and their religious superiors, but by
>   the same "independence" I am today required to at-
> tack the representative of the Holy Father. Tomorrow
> I shall perhaps be forced to attack the representative
> of Jesus Christ, the Holy Father. The following day why
> should I not then be constrained to attack God Himself?
>
> Since the government has time and again insisted that
> they are not forcing us, but simply directing us, then
> I ought only to speak from my heart, and not have said
> 'yes' with my life, and 'no' in my heart. I ought only
> to sign those declarations to which I sincerely consent
> and not affix my name to those with which I disagree.
> If I live by deceit and fear death, I become a completely
> untrustworthy man, of use to no one...
>
> I make these statements now being of a sane mind and I
> avow that whatever I may say later in a state of confu-
> sion will be entirely invalid. I am a Catholic and
> desire to love both my country and my religion. I do
> not wish discord between the two, but if the government
> cannot work harmoniously with religion, persecution will
> follow and many victims will be demanded from among Cath-
> olics. In such an event it is better that I die right
> now. (Cary-Elwes:272-4)

Father Tong was arrested and has not been heard of since.
His is the kind of language Thomas Moore would understand.

Recent reports on Catholics and Protestants in the PRC stress an extraordinary vitality, and even seem to confirm the old adage that "the blood of martyrs is the seed of Christians."

Personally I feel that the number of Catholics in the PRC has sharply declined, from some 3-million before Mao to perhaps not more than 500.000 at present. But this figure is far from certain. And there is no way of knowing what would happen if the constitutional freedom of religion, rather than serve as a tool of propaganda, becomes a fact of life.

If and when that happens, on the basis of historic precedents, one may expect a wave of sympathy for those whom history destroyed. Perhaps when that time comes, thousands of Chinese students will have returned from abroad with a much better knowledge of Christianity than their parents could ever have. It is even possible that political currents will start playing a healing role. At this writing the Chinese press is up in arms against the Russian invasion of Afghanistan. This might lead to a re-examination of a type of communism which has inexorably persecuted the Church.

At that occasion, if it is true, as many experts think, that Chinese Communism is more Chinese than communist, then the innate common sense of the Chinese people, in which their government largely shares, might awaken them to the fact that, without more freedom of expression, without more respect for religion as one of man's most treasured avenues to goodness, truth and beauty, communism is but another glorified name for oppression. Obviously, under the best of circumstances, such a process of change will take time. It may not start at the top, but at the grassroos level; it may not start in the North, but in the South where contact with the outside world is already creating new living patterns.

If and when this change comes up at the horizon, Christians can only play a minor role; a role, indeed, so insignificant that it would be preposterous for the government to fear their influence on the course of events. Christians in China are only one-thousandth of the population and they are decimated sheep without a shepherd. Their only weight is the weight of their faith: they believe that the Lord has the whole country in his hand.

But I have wandered away from the topic of this chapter. Let's get back to Catholic life in China. Obviously, the country is so large and so diverse, and our information is so spare, that no one could know all the facts. Hence, the details which follow are but a few tiny pebbles thrown at the Great Wall of our ignorance.

From within the hazy perspectives of that ignorance, I predict a more realistic attitude towards religion, and an unperceptibly slow increase of tolerance, particularly in the larger cities, and in some privileged rural sectors where Christianity has since long taken root and has the sympathy of the people. In other words, I expect to see some relaxation of that amiable pressure which prevents Catholics from abroad, such as Bishop Moser, from meeting with Catholics in China. Such a relaxation will come about without the benefit of official and legal fanfare. From January 1, 1980, when the new Penal Code goes into effect, the new tolerance could be fanned by the many Christian visitors from abroad who will keep asking questions about the nature of religious freedom in the PRC.

Dignitaries, such as the King of the Belgians who plans to visit Beijing this coming June, might feel uncomfortable at a Patriotic Mass. It would be unthinkable for the government to refuse them the priest of their choice.

There might be no acceptable Patriotic candidates for the episcopal sees now vacant. Rather than consecrate "a hundred bishops," as Father Wei suggests the government might do, the Beijing authorities might realize that they would score heavily with public opinion around the world and, for good measure, give a black eye to Russia, by loyally implementing the Constitution in the matter of human rights. Whether Paragraph 46 be amended, and the clause on "freedom to spread atheism" be thrown out of the text, that is of no importance. What really counts is the interpretation of the freedom clause in actual daily life. To quote Mao: "We must learn from facts," also in matters of religious freedom.

Meanwhile more historic temples in Beijing, Nanjing, Shanghai, Hangzhow, Suzhou, Kuilin and other scenic places will be opened to the tourist trade. In some of these temples, there are already a few real Buddhist monks who believe what they preach. As Mr Zhao Fusan has told me in Chicago, "the opening of Christian churches must wait another three to four years." In quite a few of these former churches, soldiers are quartered, and, as was the case of the cathedral of Changshun, even orders from Beijing, thrice repeated, could not dislodge them within foreseeable time.

In Canton, the Catholic cathedral was opened for the first time on Christmas 1978. It also profited from the government's loving care. The statue of the Immaculate Conception on the right side altar, which had been smashed during the Cultural Revolution, was re-installed in its former place at government expense.

Strange things could happen on the way to Tianenmen and
to the Forum. Many hotels and restaurants in the major
cities which cater to the tourist trade had Christmas trees
in their foyers. A visiting priest in Shanghai was asked
to lend a helping hand: no one at his hotel had ever seen a
Christmas tree. The PRC Embassy at Rome sent an invitation
to all priests of Chinese nationality to come and celebrate
the Chinese New Year. The Embassy was most thoughtful: should
they be embarrassed in the company of other communist invi-
tees, a separate party reserved for Catholic clergy could
easily be arranged. What price, Chinese courtesy?

+
+   +
+

We have now more and more accurate news on Catholic life
in the local communities. It would be misleading to call
any of these communities "underground churches," as some
reporters have done. There is nothing underground any place
in China, except the mines. Police know everybody by name.

Fact is, however, that police and neighbors do no longer
mind if Christians join for quiet prayer. In this matter,
Catholics are at an unmistakable advantage because Protestants, when they meet, have an irrepressible yen to sing
their hallowed hymns. Thereby they disturb the neighbors,
which is a crime punishable by law with a maximum sentence
of seven years imprisonment. Let them beware!

Catholics, whenever possible, meet for prayer, even at an
ungodly hour, as did Father Wei. They help one another,
financially and spiritually. They are developing new and
yet old ministries, such as visits to the sick and dying.

In work camps, Catholics are known for their joy and peace
of mind. The Cultural Revolution destroyed their books and
statues. Whatever texts they now possess were mostly copied
by hand, much as Japanese Catholics used to do during 250
years of persecution. Since centuries, Chinese Catholics
have shown an ardent devotion to Mary. They carry a rosary
on their person. They pray the Ave, Ya-wu Maliya uncessantly.
Surely, their theology and their devotional practices are
pre-Vatican II. But why should they change? Much better for
them to wait until they can emerge in the fullness of communion with the Pope, with their bishop, and with one another.

But that does not mean that Catholics take things lying
down. They are not"like moths flying toward the flame"飞蛾扑火.
There is a sully stonewalling at obvious vexations. A Hong

Kong priest writes that he knows of a mother with three
children who flatly refused to be sterilized. The same
priest tells of signs and wonders. Above all, he claims,
Catholics are unshakable in their faith. (Echos de la Rue
du Bac, May: 155-9)

While I was in Hong Kong a few months ago, a Catholic lady
from our former missions in Mongolia arrived on a visit to
relatives. She told us many things of interest which I have
freely strewn over these pages. But I'll never forget her
last remark: "Catholics in Hong Kong know their faith better
than we do; but we love our faith more than they do. With
all their freedom, why aren't they more fervent?"

THE LIMITS OF THE NEW CHINA

Maoism, even though it may have liberated China from the
"four old men," has not liberated it from the one we call
"the old one par excellence," certainly the oldest one of
all, the one from which we must be liberated if we want
the other liberations to have meaning: we refer to death.

Mao praised Comrade Bethune because he gave his life for
the Chinese people in the most unselfish way. We join in
this praise and admiration. The fact still remains that
Comrade Bethune, although he contributed to the victory of
the Revolution, did not take part in it and, what is more
serious, even those who are taking part in it will have to
die one day.

What meaning, then, attaches to the immense effort made by
the Chinese people to establish a more just society, if
one day those who have seen the victory must vanish and,
with few exceptions, without leaving any trace? The liberation which Mao has given to the Chinese people does
not mean much, if he does not also give them this. But
he cannot give them this liberation, the most important
liberation of all.

Christianity is essentially a religion of salvation that
maintains the incarnation, death and resurrection of the
Son of God. This readmits humanity into God's friendship,
enabling it to participate in his intimacy and find in the
community of salvation, which is the Church, eternal life
through the resurrection of the body. It is this which
Mao needs in order that the effort made by him and the
whole Chinese people may take on its full meaning.

Domenico Grasso in Chu:109

CONCLUSION:

"EYES THAT HAVE BEEN WASHED"

_____

_____

   Time has come for us to pull a few things together. This
much is certain: we have still much to learn in China; we
have still much to learn from China. How true this proverb:
"It takes a long road to know a horse's strength, and a
long time to see a man's heart." 路遥知马力、日久见人心.

   This is so much the more true that the road which Church
and China travel is bound to be a Long March on which only
the valiant shall survive. The survival of the fittest!

How much we hope and pray that Christians may find strength
in their faith, as 1 Peter 4:13 exhorts them

   that they not be bewildered by the fiery ordeal that is
   upon you, as though it were something extraordinary. It
   gives you a share in Christ's sufferings, and that is
   cause for joy; and when his glory is revealed, your joy
   will be triumphant.

   If Christ's name is flung in your teeth as an insult,
   count yourselves happy, because then that glorious
   Spirit which is the Spirit of God is resting upon you.
   If you suffer, it must not be for murder, theft, or sorcery, nor for infringing the rights of others. But if
   anyone suffers as a Christian, he should feel it no
   disgrace, but confess that name to the honor of God.

   Hence it is with great reverence that I address myself
to all Catholics, and indeed, to all Christians in the PRC,
who have suffered for their faith.

CHINA DEMYTHOLOGIZED, CHINA REMYTHOLOGIZED

To people from outside, post-Gang-of-Four China is China
demythologized. But at this stage, there is no way of telling whether what is exposed is China as it is or China re-
mythologized.

In both, arising from different assumptions and heading
for different dreams, there is restraint in making judgment,
there is hope mixed with anxiety, in responding to China in
the new situation. There is uncertainty in the Christian
response because there is uncertainty in the post-Gang-of-
Four China. And, I suspect, from the inside as well, as I
happen to be among those who believe that China demythologized is China minus its identity. The uncertainty in the
Christian response has also to do with the idea, encouraged
by China, that our non-China experience, especially western-
oriented values and tools, is not a liabilitybut an asset
in understanding China. While this privilege seems to offer
a comfortable anchorage, it somehow fails to work in the
field as visitors, Christians and otherwise, tour China in
unprecedented numbers.

While China demythologized is a China difficult to understand and respond to, the China religious situation offers
a different picture to those from outside. Although part
and parcel of China's modernization program, the more libe-
ral religious policies and their consequences are perceived
as the emergence of a visible identity. This makes response
easy, indeed, invites it. And the Christian community outside China responds.

What we have been responding to is minimally simple:
Christians in China saying very clearly: "We exist. And we
are here." But other than that, there is practically no
content. The same can be said of our response: visits,
friendly conversation, importing a few Bibles and devotional
literature, some failed attempts to re-establish missionary
activities. Under the circumstances, maybe no other kind of
response is called for. We just don't know any other. We
just don't know what the Church in China stands for. We just
don't know what role the Church in China has to play in the
meaning of the nation. Some of the leading Christian figures
in China in recent months have been trying to say that
Christians in China have succeeded in winning the fight to
exist as a Chinese Church. Here there is a little more content than mere existence. But we still do not know if it
is a myth in the sense of make-believe, or in the sense of
being part of the mythic drama of China which sums up the
significance and direction of the Chinese people.

Raymond Fong, Background Paper, "Christian Response to the New Situation," Meeting of The Ecumenical China Study Liaison Group, Brugge, 3-6
September 1979

An Open Letter to All Catholics in the PRC, January 1, 1980

Dear Brothers and Sisters in the Lord,

A Happy New Year to you all, a Christian New Year as well as a Chinese New Year!

I have no qualifications for sending you this letter as I remember what Confucius said long ago in the Analects: "When I see three people walking on the street, I know for sure that one of them could be my master." 三人行、必有我師.

All of you could be my masters: you could teach me all I have to know about the Lord Jesus Christ. Because you suffered so much more for him than I, you know him so much better than I do. I reverence you, and I admire you, because as one of your proverbs says: "Eyes that have been washed with bitter water are the brightest." 用苦水洗过的眼睛最亮.

I know you are extremely inquisitive about the outside world, as you have always been throughout your history. You want to know how other Christians look upon your situation and what they would do if they were standing in your place. Although I cannot hope to pierce the bamboo curtain behind which you hide, let me very humbly try to phrase a preliminary answer to your questions.

You need no longer be content to live on the margin of Chinese society. Our religion is now a legitimate organization, i.e., it is recognized by the Constitution and protected by the new Penal Code which goes into effect today.

Your government even puts its hopes in your collaboration. After the country was almost run to ground by the evil Gang of Four, the government is now totally absorbed in the Four Modernizations and wants to strain every nerve of every person so you might one day be citizens of one of the greatest and happiest nations on earth. The government repeatedly has asked for your help, irrespective of your faith. As Vice-premier Deng has wisely said: "The government does not mind whether a cat is white or black as long as it catches mice." And at another occasion, he also said: "The government does not care what people believe, as long as they work hard and keep the law." All this goes to show that you have entered into a new era in which religious freedom has become a fact, in which you are no longer "non-persons" as under the evil Gang of Four, and in which any official who wantonly deprives you of your constitutional rights will face harsh sentencing as provided in the Penal Code.

We who watch you from the other side of the Great Wall
that has divided us for so long, we realize that it will
not be easy for you to be totally involved in the great
task of reconstruction all the while remaining totally
Chinese and totally Christian. You are engaged in one of
the most crucial experiments in the history of China and of
the Church. Not only your future as Chinese and as Christians
but the future of us all is very much at stake. Hence we
count on you!

In your daily contacts with your countrymen please be very
sensitive to the fact that, from childhood, more than 500
million of them have been reared in hatred for our faith.
To be understood by them -- and they have the right to understand you -- you must use their language which is Marxist
language.

Your friends will tell you all about the collusion of the
Church with imperialism. They feel they have a point of
great importance; and you must take this very seriously.
You know from your own experience that Maoists are little
interested in theoretical discussions but, as Chairman Mao
has said, "theory must give way to practice." I for one like
this approach, although I realize that it puts the burden
squarely on your shoulders: It is for you to prove that you
give to Caesar what is Caesar's and to God what is God's.

You may not yet have seen the Acts of Vatican II. But the
Council issued a document, Gaudium et Spes, which, in No.
21, bids Catholics "to work -- also with atheists -- for the
rightful betterment of this world." The Council tells us
that "such an ideal cannot be realized without sincere and
prudent dialogue." Should you have an occasion for such
dialogue, you might then want to recall the famous distinction laid down by John XXIII in his Encyclical Pacem in Ter-
ris, No. 158-9: "One must never confuse error and the person
who errs, not even when there is question of error, or inadequate knowledge of truth, in the moral or religious field.
It must be borne in mind, furthermore, that neither can false
philosophical teachings regarding the nature, origin, and
destiny of the universe and of man be identified with historical movements that have economic, social, cultural or
political ends, not even when those movements have originated from those teachings." While writing these lines, good
Pope John may very well have thought of China.

I want you to know that other Catholics, in circumstances
very similar to you own, have set a high example which you
might wish to follow. If only I had the space, I should be
happy to copy here for you the Open Letter of July 13, 1979,
which Archbishop Nguyen van Binh of Hanoi and his Auxiliary
Bishop Msgr Pham van Nam have sent out to the world, or also

another letter from the leaders of religious men and women
of the Archdiocese of Ho Chi Minh City, dated July 23, 1979.
It's a great pity you do not have these letters. They might
help you become even better patriots, and even better Christians.

Recently, on August 19, and again on December 22, the Holy
Father has assured you all of the affection with which all
Catholics carry you in their hearts, and of our prayers. With
the Pope, we all share in your grief of having so few opportunities to talk of your faith to your fellow citizens, and
particularly to your children who are being indoctrinated
with Marxist-Leninist-Mao Zedong Thought.

If the present difficulties notwithstanding, you should
have an opportunity to speak about the treasures which you
carry in earthen vessels, this is what you might want to say:

"The real good news for us is the news about the Kingdom
of God!"

You will then want to give full attention to all the anx-
ieties of so many people among whom you live. Stay away from
abstractions, which are very distasteful to Maoist Thought.
Your own life must be the proof of what you say.

We read in your official papers that many Chinese are per-
plexed about the meaning of life. Some even, we are told,
are disgruntled and have become cynical about the type of
human progress in which they are involved. Perhaps, when
you meet such people, you might gently suggest that, in your
own life, faith in God is not an obstacle to personal growth
but rather a source of deep joy and peace.

You might perhaps be able to prove to the satisfaction of
your listeners that you can be, as well as they are, Chinese
with the Chinese -- even in a Maoist country.

Because we realize that the problems which you face surpass
our human forces, we all count on God's grace and constantly
keep you in our prayers. We on the outside are doing all we
can so that the Church may be worthy of your great nation.

Be then of good cheer! In days of trial, remember this
proverb: "In no prairie fire do seeds perish; see their new
blades shoot forth amidst the spring breezes."

158

BIBLIOGRAPHY AND ABBREVIATIONS

All dates are 1979 unless otherwise marked
Periodicals: Month/day:page

BR, Beijing Review.

Burton, Neil C. & Charles Bettelheim, China Since Mao, New
    York and London: Monthly Review Press, 1978.

Bush, Richard C., Jr., Religion in Communist China, Nash-
    ville and New York: Abingdon Press, 1970.

Cary-Ewes, Columba, China and the Cross, London: Longmans,
    Green & Co., 1957

CF, Ching Feng, Hong Kong.

Ching, Julia, Confucianism & Christianity, A Comparative
    Study, Tokyo, New York & San Francisco: Kodansha Inter-
    national, 1977.

CN, China Notes, New York.

Concilium, Geffré & Spae, ed., China as a Challenge to the
    Church, New York: The Seabury Press, 1979. (In several
    languages)

Chu, Michael, ed., The New China: A Catholic Response, New
    York, Ramsey, Toronto:Paulist Press, 1977.

CSM, The Christian Science Monitor

CT, China Talk, Hong Kong.

Curnow, John, Report on a Visit to China, October 1978,
    privately printed, 5+3 pages.

de Villiers, Gérard, La Chine s'éveille, Paris: Plon, 1979.

der überblick, Zeitschrift für ökumenische Begegnung und
    internationale Zusammemarbeit, 1979/4.

Garaudy, Roger, Appel aux vivants, Paris: Seuil, 1979.

Jones, Francis P., ed., Documents of the Three-Self Movement,
    New York: National Council of Churches, East Asia De-
    partment, 1963.

IDOC, Idoc International, New Series, Bulletin No. 12, Decem-
    ber 1979: "China and the Churches."

IHD, Information on Human Development, Office for Human De-
    velopment of the FABC, June 1979. (Manila)

IHT, Internaional Herald Tribune

IL, Information Letter (Geneva)

Klatt, Werner, The Chinese Model, Hong Kong: Hong Kong University Press, 1965.

Laurentin, René, Chine et Christianisme, Après les occasions manquées, Paris: Desclée De Brouwer, 1977.

LF, Le Figaro.

Mission Forum, Series 8, No. 2, 1979, "China Looks Outward," Maryknoll, N.Y.: Mission Research and Planning Department.

OR, Osservatore Romano.

Patterson, George N., Christianity in Communist China, Waco and London: Word Books, 1969.

PD, People's Daily. (Beijing)

Peyrefitte, Alain, Quand la Chine s'éveillera, Paris: Fayard, 1973.

Scherer, James A., ed., Western Christianity and The People's Republic of China: Exploring New Possibilities, Report of the Midwest China Consultation, Chicago, Ill., 1979.

SFC, San Francisco Chronicle.

Tsien Tche-hao, l'Empire du Milieu retrouvé, La Chine Populaire a trente ans, Paris: Flammarion, 1979.

Whitehead, James D., Yu-ming Shaw, N.J. Girardot, eds., China and Christianity, Historical and Future Encounters, Notre Dame, Ind.: The University of Notre Dame, 1979.

"IT'S NOW TIME TO TAKE A FRESH LOOK AT 'CHINA MISTAKES'"

Ralph Covell offers seven guidelines for mission agencies concerned with the evangelization of China:

1. <u>Patience</u>. "In 1842, Christian missionaries impatiently assumed that an 'open door' for commerce and diplomacy was also an entrance for the Gospel. We are still reaping the results of this tragic action." Mission agencies need patience to develop new attitudes, new goals, new strategies and new methods. God will not be hurried and neither must we.

2. <u>Disowning of worldly power</u>. From 1842 on, "missionaries rode the coattails of political power... Mission agencies must avoid any alliance with power and privilege that would create special advantage in presenting the Gospel message."

3. <u>Contextualization</u>. For the most part, Christianity was a "foreign exotic transplant which never came to grips with the Chinese worldview." In contrast, today "the Gospel needs to be related much more thoroughly to the Chinese culture. Any new effort in China requires missionaries to adopt the primary role of learners."

4. <u>Unity</u>. We must also avoid denominational fragmentation, for, under suffering, Chinese Christians have found unity in Christ "and put no priority on man-made divisions."

5. <u>Cooperation</u>. "What degree of cooperation are evangelical agencies prepared to develop?"

6. <u>Priority on nationals' interests</u>. Outside agencies "must never forget that... God's people are already there as a spiritually lean, disciplines, committed church, molded and refined in the crucible of testing." Missionaries must be "sensitive to their needs and their precarious situation."

7. <u>Focus on hope</u>. The Gospel's advance must be rooted in a theology of hope, valid in the midst of suffering.

<u>Evangelical Mission Quarterly</u>, April 1979

INDEX

++++ AN INTERNATIONAL CHINA-BROWSER'S TREASURE (?) TROVE +

The other day, I browsed in the leftist corner of
a Leuven bookshop. Look what I found: a wealth of
interesting material more or less related to the
theme of this book. Much of this material comes
from Beijing (B), is nicely illustrated and makes
good reading. It's also very cheap or free of charge.

While I do not intend to follow any particular order in
this bibliographical catch as catch can, let's start off
with China's rulers. Houa Kouo-Feng, Successeur de Mao
Tsé-toung, Souvenirs biographiques, Paris: Editions du Centenaire, 1978. "Inconnu il y a deux ans et déjà populaire
dans le monde entier, on sait encore peu de choses de son
passé, de son cheminement, de sa personnalité profonde.
Soldat de l'Armée rouge à 17 ans, président du Parti communiste chinois à 57 ans, c'est un bon demi-siècle d'histoire qui traverse la vie de Houa Kouo-feng; une vie, un
personnage, un idéal intimement mêlés aux grands évène-
ments de la révolution chinoise." -- Houa Kouo-feng,
Poursuivons jusqu'au bout la révolution sous la dictature
du proléteriat, De l'ètude du Tome V des 'Oeuvres Choisies
de Mao Tsetoung'", B, 1977.

Tome V of Mao's Selected Works has attracted wide attention, to the point that there is a special 390-p. political
lexicon which comes to a very useful tool of interpretation:
Lexique politique de la Chine contemporaine, Paris: Ed. du
Centenaire, 1979. There are 26 entries on philosophy (
among them: atheism, theism, unity of opposites, etc.,which
we have discussed) and 11 on religion (Buddhism, Confucius,
Tao, Yin and Yang, Dalai Lama). Very useful for quick reference.

Next to Premier Hua, there is Vice-Premier Deng Xiaoping.
Vent d'est (a magazine which translates texts from the PRC
pres), No. 3, 1976, has an article "Les ouvriers contre
le programme de Deng Xiaoping," which is very critical,
while, a few years later, Chi Hsin's Teng Hsiao-ping -- A
Political Biography, Hong Kong: Cosmos Books, 1978, is an
"in-depth analysis of the question of bureaucracy and
'capitalist-roaders' in the Chinese Communist Party."

I found little on Mao himself, but so much the more on his
beloved compantion in arms, Zhou Enlai. In fact the only
livres de tendresse which I found were about Zhou:

We Will Always Remember Premier Chou En-lai, B., 1977, of
which I also found a Spanish translation Nuestro Chou En-lai
with a fine picture of Mao and Zhou taken at the 24th Session
of the Central People's Government Council, 1953. The caption
calls Mao and Zhou "los más íntimos compañeros de armas."
I was also lucky to find the French translation of William Hin-
ton's famous interviews with Zhou in 1971, published by the
Association des Amitiés Franco-Chinoises at Paris. Recently,
magazines from Beijing have vied with one another to glorify
Mao's companion. Thus la Chine en construction, May 1979,
writes about "Zhou Enlai et le Mouvement du 4 Mai," while
its sister publication China im Aufbau, also of May brings
an article on "Zhou Enlai in seiner Jugend": "Wie war das
Leben von Genossen Zhou Enlai mit den Entwicklungen in China
vor 1949 verknüpft? Mit der 4. Mai-Bewegung der antiimperi-
alistischen patriotischen Bewegung der Gründung der KPCh usw?
Unser Artikel gibt Antwort darauf."

Another livre de tendresse is that of Luxun, Un combattant
comme ça, Poèmes et Essais, présentés par Michelle Loi, Paris: Editions du Centenaire. Lu Xun, of course, is the famous
novelist whom I quoted on p. 70. The book starts with a somewhat chilling quotation from one of his books: "Pour vivre
il faut tuer, pour aimer il faut haïr -- Il faut vivre et
aimer pour écrire." Although Lu Xun had his ups and downs
with Mao, his picture has this subscript praise: "Lou Sin,
grand écrivain, grand penseur et grand révolutionnaire."

There are some books of a more scientific nature. Maria
Cristina Gibelli, Organisatie van de ruimte in China,
Amsterdam: Ekologische Uitgeverij, 1979, is the Dutch version of her Politica e organizzazione del territoro in
Cina, Rome, 1976, with her corrections of 1978. The gist
of the book is this: " Steunedn op de landbouw èn op de
industrie. Niet alleen de zware industrie ontwikkelen,
maar ook kleinschalige projekten in iedere plaats. De tegen-
stellinge opheffen tussen stad en platteland."

Chinese history is being rewritten in a new book on a subject that fuels certain aspects of the PRC attitude toward
Christianity: La Révolution des Taiping, B., 1978, prepared
"par les camarades de la faculté d'histoire de l'Université
de Changhai." There are interesting illustrations, one of
which has this caption: "Durant la révolution des Taiping,
un bon nombre d'étrangers soutinrent héroïquement l'armée
des Taiping. En décembre 1863, un ami Anglais, Le-le, aida
l'armée des Taiping à repousser les force navales des Tsing
à Wousi, grâce à l'engagement du Firefley, bâtiment de guerre
capturé à "l'Armée toujours victorieuse."

Medical science also has its turn. I found two pamphlets on
acupuncture: Franchir le "Seuil du Mutisme" and l'Anésthésie

par acupuncture, both from Beijing. There is also a brandnew
book on general medecine and particularly on psychiatric
treatment in the PRC: Rob Vernooy, Maken de Chinesen gekheid?,
Assen: van Gorcum, 1979.

Turning to the political field, I discovered a very informa-
tive history of the Communist Party: Jacques Guillermaz, Le
Parti communiste chinois au pouvoir, Paris: Payot, 1979.
The first volume of 406 pages describes the period 1949-62,
the second volume of 380 pages brings the information up to
1979. The first volume has a cover picture of Mao, the second
volume, of Hua.

There are several editions of proceedings of National People's
Congresses, the most recent of which I have discussed in these
pages: Main Documents of the Second Session of the Fifth National People's Congress of the People's Republic of China, B.,
1979, with the opening speech of Ye Jianying, and also his
closing address. (See p. 19 and 21)

Obviously, no collection would be complete without some vigorous criticism of the evil Gang of Four, and of Lin Biao
and Confucius. I found in my Leuven bookshop: Tchen Yong-
kouei, Critiquer à fond la Bande des Quatre et imprimer un
nouvel essor à la généralisation des districts de type
Tatchai, B., 1977, and Critique de Lin Piao et de Confucius (pi-Lin pi-Kong, Janvier-décembre 1974, Lausanne: Alfred
Eibel, 1975.

There are finally illustrated books, such as Demokratisch
socialisme in China, Berchem: E.P.O., 1978, being a trave-
logue by a Belgian group through rural China, and Lu Hsün,
Der Grosse Revolutionär, Denker und Schriftsteller whom I
have already mentioned.

Page 4 of this book has a Prayer for China and the Church,
written when the earthquake at Tangshan was announced. My
attention was therefore attracted to a little book, Tangshan
au lendemain du tremblement de terre, B., 1976. I also said
something about Chinese universities and students. More can
be read about them in another booklet: Een proletariese universiteit, De ervaringen van de Tsinghua-universiteit in Peking na de kulturele revolutie, Rotterdam: Stichting Onder-
zoek en Studie, 1970.

My Leuven red bookshop is very objective in listing its source material. You'll soon find there cheeck to jowl two Catholic priests: Michel Schooyans, La provocation chinoise,
Paris: Editions du Cerf, 1973, and Joseph J. Spae, Church
and China: Towards Reconciliation? ... But that's another
story.

By the same author:

Itō Jinsai, A Philosopher, Educator and Sinologist of the Tokugawa Period,
    Monumenta Serica, Monograph Series, Peiping, 1948, and Paragon
    Book Reprint Corporation, New York, 1967.

Catholicism in Japan, International Institute for the Study of Religions,
    Tokyo, 2nd revised ed., 1964.

Christian Corridors to Japan, Oriens Institute, 2nd revised ed., 1968.

Christianity Encounters Japan, Oriens Institute, 1968.

Christians of Japan, Oriens Institute, 1970.

Japanese Religiosity, Oriens Institute, 1971.

Shinto Man, Oriens Institute, 1972.

Buddhist-Christian Empathy, Oriens Institute & The Chicago Institute of
    Theology and Culture, 1980.